STEP
ON
FEAR

DR CATHERINE YANG

STEP ON FEAR

First published in 2020 by Dean Publishing
PO Box 119
Mt. Macedon, Victoria, 3441
Australia
deanpublishing.com

Copyright © Dr. Catherine Yang

All rights reserved. No part of this publication may be reproduced, stored in a retrieval system or transmitted in any way or by any means, electronic, mechanical, photocopying, recording or otherwise, without the prior written permission from the publisher and author.

Cataloguing-in-Publication Data
National Library of Australia
Title: Step On Fear
Edition: 1st edn
ISBN: 978-1-925452-27-3
Category: Self-help/Memoir/Business

The information provided in this book is designed to provide helpful information on the subjects discussed. This book is not meant to be used, nor should it be used, to diagnose or treat any physical, emotional or psychological medical condition. For diagnosis or treatment of any medical problem, consult your own physician. The publisher and author are not responsible for any specific health or psychological needs that may require medical supervision and are not liable for any damages or negative consequences from any treatment, action, application or preparation, to any person reading or following the information in this book. References are provided for informational purposes only and do not constitute endorsement of any websites or other sources. Neither the publisher nor the individual author(s) shall be liable for any physical, psychological, emotional, financial, or commercial damages, including, but not limited to, special, incidental, consequential or other damages. Our views and rights are the same: You are responsible for your own choices, actions, and results.

TO MY PARENTS
*for raising me to believe that the future
belongs to those with dreams.*

AND TO MY HUSBAND AND CHILDREN
for making our dreams come true.

AND TO OUR GOD ALMIGHTY
for affirming that the truth will set you free!

CONTENTS

Introduction ix

Part 1: Finding My Smile Across The Miles 1

Part 2: The Other Side Of Fear 25

Part 3: S.T.E.P. On Fear 59

Part 4: S.T.E.P. On Fear *Teams* 123

Acknowledgements 171

About The Author 173

Testimonials 175

Notes 179

Endnotes 181

INTRODUCTION

I remember the first day I walked into the beautiful, hygienic clinic. The benches were spotless and the sparkling floor reflected my face. It was very different from the medical clinics that I had seen. No one was coughing and spluttering or hugging their ailing body and moaning. I eyed the couple that ran the clinic, their warm and smiling faces made the room even brighter. Their happiness and joy radiated through the clinic and I immediately felt content and safe within their presence.

I was 12 years old at the time. My hard-working parents were from a small country village in Pingtung in the southernmost part of Taiwan. Taiwan was formerly called 'Ilha Formosa' meaning beautiful island in Portuguese from when the Portuguese sailors first spotted the quaint island back in 1542 and recorded it on their maps.

My parents moved around a lot in constant search of a better life for my brother and me. After years of living in different homes on the outskirts of Taipei, they eventually managed to get an apartment in Taipei, and that's where I grew up.

This particular day, I was the lucky one. This was a day my parents had saved hard for. They had enough savings for one child's orthodontic braces and follow-up treatment, and I was chosen. I couldn't believe my good fortune. The little country girl had just stepped into the cleanest environment she had ever seen and was being treated like royalty.

I loved everything about that moment. The clinic, the kind clinicians and how special I felt. It never occurred to me then that some people were scared of dentists. I wasn't. I was in awe. I decided right then and there that I didn't want to do what my parents and relatives did. I didn't want to follow traditional family occupations. I wanted to pave my own path; to be special.

I wanted to be a dentist. I wanted to be the best and kindest dentist. I wanted to be the first dentist in my family. The idea ignited inside of me like an unwavering flame of desire.

This calling only grew stronger each time I went for my regular visits to adjust my braces. I could feel the contentment and happiness in their clinic. The couple was always smiling and courteous to every patient. I watched them welcome people into the dental clinic like everyone was family. Every patient waited contently without any complaint. The couple worked with true love, passion and care and their safe and healthy environment was like living inside a beautiful picture book.

I didn't realise the impact their whole-hearted manner had on me until a decade or so later. I guess that's what can happen with defining moments in life, it's often only in hindsight that we see the extent of someone's true and lasting impact.

INTRODUCTION

I have since built my life on this philosophy, inspired to sprinkle smiles and love in the hope that my actions and care also help shape others in a positive and inspirational light.

Catherine is sharing more in her INTERACTIVE book.

See exclusive behind-the-scenes videos, audios and photos.

DOWNLOAD it now at
deanpublishing.com/steponfear

> If you see someone
> without a smile,
> give them one of yours.

PART ONE

Finding My Smile Across The Miles

> The enemy is fear.
> We think it is hate;
> but it is fear.
>
> **GANDHI**

THE DISCOVERY OF FEAR

Like most people, I have known struggle. It's part of the human condition. Our history books are full of stories and facts about humans' struggle for a better life. In many ways, we all strive for our unique definition of what constitutes a 'better' or more 'fulfilled' life. It's in our pursuit of happiness and overcoming the impending obstacles, that we discover our depth and inner resources.

Throughout my journey, I've discovered that there is one major thing that can stall and block a person's progress. Something that can force even the strongest minds into submission and surrender. Something that can prevent even the most charming and charismatic people from shining bright. That thing is *fear*.

Yes, fear seems to play a greater role in our life than we want it to. In fact, if we don't learn how to deal with it effectively, it can control our life and steer us away from our dreams, desires and pursuits.

My first true encounter with fear came at a young age. My parents had a very serious fight and I started to imagine all sorts of wild scenarios in my mind. I imagined losing the safety of my home and having to choose between my parents. I imagined being in dire poverty and being separated from my brother. Fear became such a big part of my life that I began to try and mend my parents' arguments.

My parents grew up in the poor area of Taiwan, and so their entire lives had been dedicated to providing a better standard of living for their own children. Though I didn't understand the pressures at the time this aim became embedded in our family culture and we bonded over sharing this same beautiful vision; a future vision of contentment and peace. A vision where my parents didn't have to work so hard and their children had every possible opportunity available to them.

Their arguments started to shake our dream, and my foundations. Until then, I thought that I had the perfect family, the best family in the world. We were a family with a vision. My mum and dad were my safe haven and I didn't want anything to burst my bubble. The first time I heard them yell and use the word 'divorce', it was as if my perfect glass bubble shattered into a million tiny pieces. All of a sudden, my beautiful utopian world was falling apart.

My mind went into shock and I told myself, *I'm fine, I'm fine, I'm fine,* as if I was trying to brainwash myself into believing it. I began to write down a song that was originally written by American playwright John Howard Payne and composed by Englishman Henry Rowley Bishop in the 19th Century.

The song 'Home Sweet Home' was translated into Mandarin with the same beautiful tune. Though I didn't know the English version at the time, I kept writing the lyrics of the Mandarin version over and over again. My pencil was scribbling onto the page as rapidly as my heartbeats were thumping in my chest.

Mid pleasures and palaces though we may roam,
Be it ever so humble, there's no place like home;
A charm from the skies seems to hallow us there,
Which, seek thro' the world, is ne'er met with elsewhere.

Home, home, sweet, sweet home,
There's no place like home;
O, there's no place like home.

I gaze on the moon as I tread the drear wild,
And feel that my mother now thinks of her child;
As she looks on that moon from our own cottage door,
Thro' the woodbine whose fragrance shall cheer me no more.

An exile from home, splendor dazzles in vain,
O, give me my lowly thatched cottage again;
The birds singly gaily that came at my call;
Give me them, and that peace of mind, dearer than all.[1]

— John Howard Payne & Henry Rowley Bishop —

---

1 Russell, Bertrand. *Unpopular Essays*. (1950), George Allen & Unwin, London.

I wrote out the lyrics like my life depended on them, and then wrote a full-page letter to each parent and included the lyrics of the song. I didn't talk about their fight; I wrote how thankful and blessed I was to have such a lovely family. I wrote that I just want to share this beautiful song with them so whenever they thought of the song, they would feel the same. I couldn't stop singing the song, it replayed over and over again in my mind like a continuous record stuck on play.

Mum and Dad had locked themselves into separate rooms within our tiny apartment. I finished each letter in my best handwriting and slid one letter under each door. I could hear sobbing as I kneeled carefully down to deliver my special notes and then tiptoed back away to pray. *Oh God, please help us. Please keep my parents together. Please help them read my letter and feel that there's no place like home!*

After a couple of hours, they came out of their rooms and the next day it was like the fight never occurred. Nobody talked about it. In my innocent mind, I thought that my magic song and letter worked like a charm. I was too young to understand that if couples do not deal with the conflicts in the relationship, they just come back like a boomerang.

So they started arguing once again. Over time, I became used to their style of arguing. I started to see the patterns and most importantly, I began to see how fear can stop people from living fully. I began to notice that adults had lots of fears too. I slowly began to recognise fear within myself and the endless hours I spent trying anything and everything to *not* have fear in my life.

I began to see how living in fear was exhausting for the spirit and how destructive it was to dreams. I began to see that sharing your fears reduced them but holding onto them and trying to ignore them only ended badly.

FEAR OF THE UNKNOWN

When I was in primary school, my parents started to take us to a local church group founded by a Christian lady called Dr Doris Brougham. The church group had a Youth Rally every Saturday night organised by Overseas Radio & Television Inc.[2]

Dad began to learn English from their Studio Classroom[3] and listen to their beautiful songs. He went to church solely for the purpose of learning English. As we didn't know English, he felt that it would be great to learn. The people at church were so nice and friendly that it seemed like a wonderful combination. So every weekend, we travelled by two or three buses and after an hour or so we ended up at church.

I instantly loved it. Despite growing up in traditional Chinese culture, we embraced Christianity. Mum and Dad allowed my brother and I to choose whatever we wanted for ourselves. I could see the battle of faith going on inside my parents. They wanted to accept a new Christian religion without upsetting their extended Chinese family or being perceived as bringing disgrace to their traditional family beliefs.

Fear of the unknown or fear of what other people may think can often drive us from our true heart's calling. Fear of stepping outside cultural norms and being different can stop us from living our best lives. It happens in many families across many different cultures.

In the following chapters, we will explore *your* fears and give you the right tools and techniques to overcome them. We will identify what you're afraid of, discover what your heart calls for and question what stops you from moving forward in your life.

---

2   Dr Dorothy Brougham http://www.ortv.com/en/dr-doris-brougham

3   Studio Classroom http://www.studioclassroom.com/h_doris.php

THE UNKNOWN CONTINUES

In pursuit of a better life for us my parents decided to take yet another extraordinary leap into the unknown and immigrate to Australia. They felt that the educational system in Taiwan was no longer suitable for their children. We were really burnt out.

Although I very much enjoyed school and loved to learn, I didn't like the competition. The school system in Taiwan was super competitive and demanding. It was an around-the-clock to-do list of getting to school early to sit exams, write papers, compete in trials and keep high grades. We had to get up around 6am to catch the bus and upon arrival at school we had to sit down and without even a "Hello", an exam paper was shoved under our nose, "Begin!"

We always began with a test and the learn-at-all-costs theme continued throughout the day. Students in eighth grade had to stay longer and keep learning. We had to stay until 5 or 6pm, often later. So by the time we arrived home, it was very late. Then we had to study and do homework; it was just like a never-ending rat race over and over again.

Until finally it happened — I burnt out. I couldn't even remember anything I had learned. My whole furious learning capacity had reached boiling point and seized.

Thankfully on the weekends, Dad would take us out to the park or we'd do some fun community work with the church. My brother had never really liked mainstream education, so many times he'd stop at a park to play on the way home from school, often worrying my parents of his whereabouts. But without these outlets and activities, the schooling system seemed designed to wear students down into a pit of exhaustion.

When I was 15 and Eric was 14, my parents began the immigration process to Australia. It was exceptionally hard to meet all the criteria. It was a very big decision because it meant my parents had to sell everything they owned, everything they had worked for their entire lives. We spoke very little English and didn't know life outside of Taiwan. We came to Australia with my parents' life savings, which barely helped us buy a house. The rest of the money was spent on Eric's and my education.

Dad started a small business selling computer parts as computers had just entered the market and started to capture some attention in business. His very limited English was a struggle. Dad bought a little Toyota Cressida and would drive every day to visit potential clients all over Sydney just to see if they would be interested in buying some computer parts. He would look through the Yellow Pages to try and read English. He would scan the pages for businesses that might require computer parts and go and visit them one by one.

He would study the old *Gregory Street Directory* at night and plan his trips for the next day, bookmarking and photocopying pages and marking the route with highlighter. Often, he'd take his car and do a dry run the day before making sure he knew the way for the next day. As his English was limited, he'd write sales scripts and practise them out loud.

It wasn't unusual for him to drive hundreds of kilometres in a day just in the mere hope of a potential sale. He did this day in and day out for the entire week, just to make ends meet in a new and foreign country. We could see the sacrifices he made and I often questioned life. It made me wonder: what is life really about? Is life one sacrifice after another?

I began to wonder if my parents were happy and what I could do to pay them back. I began to wonder about needing money versus almost killing yourself to get it and if it was worth it or not. I didn't know the answer — yet.

I wondered how many generations just followed the same ideas of their parents, feeling the need to work hard to get ahead. I started to question if my dad didn't like the lifestyle that he had; did I want to follow his footsteps? Where did happiness fit into striving for better?

Was the right decision to sacrifice your happiness for the sake of others? What would happen if you made a different decision? These questions swirled around in my mind as we were thrust into a new country and disorientated by uncertainty.

I began to ponder the bigger questions in life. I wondered if I would be happy and what kind of opportunities this new life would bring me. I began to soul search deeply, to question life's true meaning and ask the pressing questions: why do I exist? What am I going to do with my life?

I uncovered what I first found out as that little girl desperate for her parents to stay together, by examining human emotion and behaviour. I started to notice that whenever I was in doubt, or felt sad or frustrated, there was always a factor of fear present.

As a new girl in a new city with nothing but a dream, I could clearly see how fear could paralyse me. Fear had the power to manipulate my mind and persuade me to not try. But I couldn't let fear stop me. Dad didn't let fear stop him. I had to find a way.

THE SIGHT OF NEW SHORES

> *"You cannot discover new oceans unless you have the courage to lose sight of the shore."*
> — **André Gide** —

When I first came to Australia at the tender age of 15, I came armed with only two English responses, "Bye" (with a wave) and "Fine thank you, and you?"

Whenever people would say, "Hello, how are you?" my standard answer was always, "Fine, thank you, and you?"

Even if someone said, "Have a wonderful day," I would say, "Fine thank you, and you?"

I never knew how to reply to people's questions, whether it was our neighbours, people in the shopping centre or at the school bus stop. Even after my first year at public school I was still at the level of, "Fine, thank you, and you?" I imagined how mortified my parents would be if they found out that after all their blood, sweat and tears, I hadn't progressed from that simple greeting.

I would hide and eat lunch by myself at school so no one tried to speak to me. I didn't think that I should sit around and eat lunch in a social setting like the other kids, chatting, laughing and socialising. I knew that my parents had worked too hard to have me picnic every day at school, so instead I sat on the library steps eating and studying without making eye contact with anyone.

My parents continued to strive for more and soon moved me to a private school. So I attended Pymble Ladies' College in Year 11 and 12. It was my second year in Australia, and I was working as hard as I could in a foreign language. I knew that somehow I would have to sit my final exams in a mere two years' time and my anxiety around this was at an all-time high. How on earth could I take exams in English when I had barely grasped the language? The thought made me shudder.

To add insult to injury, I soon learned that my newly arrived status and poor English-speaking skills would get me no special consideration or exemptions for the exams. I was panic-stricken! It felt like mission impossible and I wanted to cry and never stop. But I didn't let them fall. There was no time for tears.

Every day I saw what my parents sacrificed to give me these opportunities. I felt a huge sense of responsibility to them, so I gave myself no permission to speak anything other than English. I had to limit my native tongue and plunge myself into English at any opportunity. I again used my lunchtimes as studying time (with some quick bites of food).

Soon one of the teachers at the College blew my cover. She found me sitting alone and to my surprise she knew my name. I didn't even know her. She said, "Catherine, what are you doing here? Why are you sitting all by yourself?" I pretended to smile and tried to say in my best English that I wanted to eat by myself.

She said, "I know you are new to school. Can I please introduce you to a group of very nice people?" I didn't want to be disrespectful, so I agreed.

She walked me over to a group of my very first Aussie friends. She said their names but I only remembered their smiles and how nice they were. As they were all 100% Aussie born and bred, they didn't speak any other language. This was precisely what I needed, and they were kind enough to teach me. We had all chosen different subjects so I didn't get their help in the classroom but it was nice to feel a sense of belonging.

Over time, I was fortunate to have many different people help me in class. I had my class helpers and my new lunchtime friends — a good nurturing environment.

But something kept lingering like a plague in my soul — I couldn't enjoy my newfound friendships as much as I wanted to. I had to stay focused. I had to study. I had to learn English very well in a super short time and pass my schooling. No special consideration!

Even though I was deeply touched by the beauty of friendship and human kindness, I couldn't fully enjoy it. In Taiwan, I was brought up in such a way that I thought I just had to study. Study hard, study more and study often. I found myself often haunted by this idea and didn't allow myself to socialise with my friends outside of school.

There were a lot of extra activities offered at the school called 'optionals', which cost extra money. I knew my parents couldn't afford any of them and I didn't want them to feel bad. So whenever a notice about a forthcoming ski trip or field trip came up, I read the notes myself and quickly threw them away.

I remember one time I got off the bus and began walking home, tears streaming down my face. My friends were all away together on an 'optional weekend trip' and I had made an excuse not to go. I couldn't allow myself to have fun in case I failed. I couldn't afford to miss a whole weekend of study or ask my parents for money. I cried the entire walk home, aching that I couldn't be on the trip with my friends.

At the time, I was naïve enough to believe that I could cry out all my tears so they would be all used up and there wouldn't be any left. I composed myself before walking into the house, as I knew Mum was going to ask about my day. When she did, I answered, "Fantastic!" in my best English and with my best fake smile.

FAILING FORWARD

Despite my all-consuming English study, I failed my first English exam. I didn't see it as just failing an exam; I saw it as being 'a failure'. I had worked day and night, sacrificed all my spare time and was left with a big fat fail.

Science was even worse. I got a zero! I didn't even know zero was a score. I remember my science teacher handing back all the corrected papers and I heard students whispering their scores — some said 70 per cent, someone said 96 per cent and the lowest score that I heard (besides mine) was 50 per cent. Mine wasn't even a score. Panic rose inside of me, threatening to strangle my dreams. *Oh no, I'm going to break my parents' hearts; they're going to feel so sad. What can I do now?*

I felt ashamed, not because of the marks necessarily but for when people asked my parents, "How are your children going at school?" I didn't want them to feel ashamed because of me. I couldn't bear that. I tried hard to keep self-doubt from devouring my optimism. I prayed hard and studied even harder. I owed them that. I couldn't afford another bad score. I couldn't afford to fail.

Lucky for me, one kind-hearted English teacher refused to give up on me. I couldn't believe what she did. The school holidays were approaching (which for me meant more studying), she said to me, "Catherine, I am going to give you a few topics to write an essay about. I know it is school holidays but I am going to give you my home address and I want you to write one essay on each topic and ask your dad to drive you to my house and put your essay in the letterbox. I will mark each essay and give you my feedback. When you do the next essay and drop it off, my marking will be in the letterbox for you."

I couldn't believe my luck and the kindness of this wonderful teacher. This was a game-changer for me. A ray of light I so desperately needed. She didn't ask for money or recognition, she simply asked that I write essays and drop them to her house. She held an unwavering love and belief in me that steered me toward my dream of passing school.

She didn't just say the school motto, *'All' Ultimo Lavoro'* which is Latin for *'strive for the highest'* — she embodied it in her actions and her kind encouraging words, an angel on Earth.

So during the school holidays I madly wrote, read and studied English, among other subjects. Dad drove me to my teacher's house where the letterbox and I exchanged our secrets. And true to her word, on my next arrival, a marked-up essay was filled with feedback, tips and corrections.

Sometimes, I still allowed myself to dream of becoming a dentist, to imagine my clean and calm environment greeting people with love and warmth. But I didn't allow too much daydreaming, that would have to wait whilst I generated essay after essay and tried to super-learn a foreign language. I was on a mission.

Every morning I filled my mind with faith. My daily ritual was followed as diligently as my studies. I would start the day by singing a hymn and offering a morning devotion. I'd read Psalms before I studied. I liked Psalms' short and beautiful verses, they'd fill me with faith and inspired me to make the best of each day. I would pray to God for my final exam score and held a secret sequence of perfect numbers in my head and heart. The numbers were my 'dream score'. I visualised them in my mind and asked the heavens to help me achieve them.

I didn't know the exact score required to get into dentistry because they changed them every year, but I knew it wasn't an average score and I'd have to aim high, higher than perhaps I was able to achieve.

With my angel teacher's tuition, I passed my next English exam. Though my marks weren't as high as others, a pass was not a fail and I felt a small surge of victory inside. Month after month, day after day, my head was in a book and my hand was writing with a frenzy of its own. My English began to improve and my English scores slowly crept higher. Each higher number was an internal celebration.

At school, some people used to think all Asian people were super smart, but I didn't feel like that at all. I knew it wasn't genetic; it was damn hard work. And my dental dream meant that I needed extremely high grades, and without a basic grasp of the English language, I would not meet the necessary requirements.

Fear kept trying to 'remind me' that I was a non-English speaker needing super-high marks to achieve my dream. Fear tried to tell me, *It's too hard. It's too far out of reach.* I had to turn away from fear and toward faith.

But fear kept pestering me, *You don't even know English like an Australian, how can you get high grades?* I turned away from fear.

But fear came back again, *You'll never make it and all of your hard work will be for nothing!*

Finally I turned to fear and said, *No!* I couldn't let fear control me or my destiny. I had to get stronger, higher and smarter than fear. I had to use it as leverage. I had to figure out how to handle fear and get good grades. I worked on both.

OPENING UP TO A NEW WORLD

In our final year of high school it was part of the curriculum to see the school's career advisor and discuss our future career paths. I felt awkward to share my wildest dream to become a dentist. I felt tentative and shy, but I confessed to Mrs D, the career advisor that my deepest dream was to become a dentist.

Surprisingly, she looked at me with a big smile and said, "Go for it Catherine, go and make this world a better place with more smiles!"

I clung to her words of encouragement like a lifeline, a rope of salvation and belief that could carry me further and higher.

I sat my Year 12 exams like a racecar driver would take to the racetrack. Full-blown laser focus with one goal in mind, to finish, to win, to be victorious. One wrong move could equal devastation. I couldn't afford one wrong move. My life vision depended on my ability to execute!

I did the best I could. I gave it my all. I used every second of exam time to read over my answers, to re-evaluate my ideas, to re-examine my efforts. *Had I done enough? Was I enough?* I didn't know. I only knew one thing: I had done my best and I hadn't let fear sabotage me. That's all I knew. I prayed it was enough.

As fate would have it, the day I was to receive my results my elderly grandfather, accompanied by my aunt and cousin, flew to visit us in Australia for the very first time. They travelled 7000kms over the Pacific Ocean to come and visit us in Sydney.

I had recently just gained my P plates and drove my little car over the Sydney Harbour Bridge for the first time and headed toward Sydney International Airport. In the pit of my stomach churned both excitement and anxiety. I was excited to see my grandfather and relatives but anxious to receive my exam results. The letterbox held secrets again.

After lots of hugs and smiles at the airport, we drove back home chatting and enjoying our drive through Sydney. As I pulled up to our house, I noticed a large white A4 envelope sticking out of our letterbox. Our letterbox held my fate.

My parents welcomed our newly arrived family into our house as I walked slowly and quietly to my room with the envelope hiding behind my back. It was hard to reconcile that what the envelope held determined the next chapter of my life.

I placed the envelope on my desk, closed my eyes and prayed with all my faith for the score I had asked God for every single day; the score that I had even used as the final three digits of my student ID code; the numbers that I had placed so much importance on that they single-handedly held my destiny.

I eyed the envelope one last time and took a deep breath. I opened the envelope slowly, no ripping or tearing. Precision hands like a dentist. As I took out the results, my breath got caught in my throat. I was in awe, in tears, in joy. It was an absolute miracle. I couldn't believe my eyes; **Catherine Yu-Ying Yang — 99.40!**

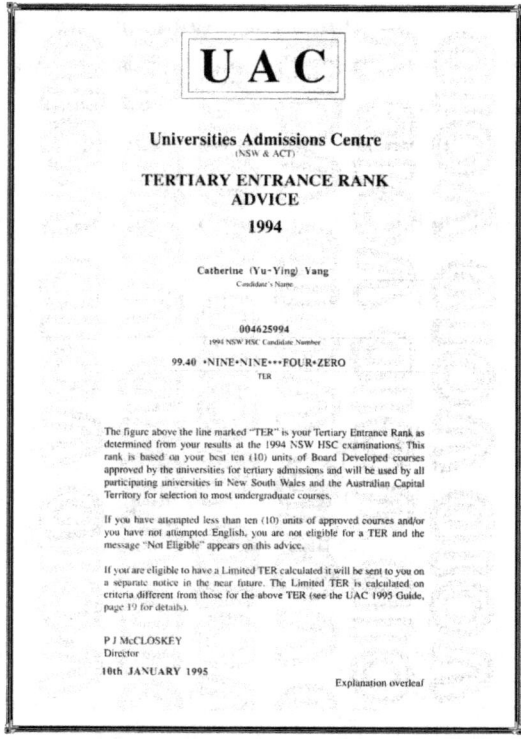

I read *my* name and *my* result. Relief dropped from my heart to my feet. The weight and pressure that I had thrust upon myself fell like cement to the floor. I didn't know my smile could stretch so far. I didn't know the numbers could mean so much or that dreams could actually come true. But they did. My dream came true, with no exemption, no special consideration. I now felt that was the best way — to achieve something that I felt was impossible without exemption or special consideration. That meant something. That meant that I did it! Me! Little Catherine Yang.

I could choose Faculty of Medicine and I knew many Asian families desperately wanted their kids to become medical doctors. It was the Holy Grail of education. But I stayed true to what I had always wanted to do. I recalled my career advisor's words about spreading smiles, and I remembered the little girl that had stepped into that clean Taiwanese clinic all those years ago.

I applied to the Faculty of Dentistry at the University of Sydney. After an interview, they offered me the Faculty of Dentistry Alumni Scholarship. I was delirious with joy — over the moon. My life had changed. Or I had changed my life.

However, I also realised something. That all my trying and effort, all my grit and determination to conquer the fears inside me and pursue my goals, had left me exhausted. I was elated with triumph but depleted from my marathon attempt to succeed. I reflected on my humble upbringing, Taiwan's cost of living and challenging school system.

I remembered the time when I was enjoying my favourite beef noodle soup on a cold winter's day at a local food stall, watching the news of a flu outbreak. The owner of the store said to me, "Poor people like us cannot afford to be sick. Expensive medical treatment is for the rich people."

On my way home, I thought to myself, *Wouldn't it be nice to make healthcare accessible to all people? Why does healthcare only belong to those who can afford it?* I silently vowed that when I reached my dream to become a dentist, I would treat people from all walks of life and I would give to those less fortunate. I held onto that vow inside my heart.

The day when I opened the envelope from the Board of Education and received the confirmation of admission into the Faculty of Dentistry in the University of Sydney, I knew that I was choosing one of the most beautiful jobs in the world. Gratitude coursed through my body and finally brought me to my knees. I was thankful for everything. I was thankful for the struggle, for the teachers, for my new Aussie friends, for my parents and brother, for my teacher's secret letterbox exams, for the chance to face all my fears.

I was grateful for all the positives and negatives, because without both I could not have found the deeper resources within to conquer the many obstacles that threatened to steer me off-course.

ENJOYING SUCCESS

The day that I received my scholarship was rather interesting. Imagine a packed auditorium with lots of proud parents. When I was called on stage to accept my award, my smile was big. If they had a video of my face when I accepted that award on the stage, you could tell that my smile was wide, but my eyes were searching the room looking for my parents in the audience. I wanted more than anything to see their happy faces because seeing their happy faces made me happy.

That's when I realised that my happiness was intertwined around my parents' happiness. I was searching for their happiness in the crowd, so desperately wanting to see them feel triumphant more than me. And though of course, I was happy to receive the award and recognition for my hard work, I wasn't allowing much of that joy in. I was looking outwards for happiness and hoping my achievement made others happy. Hoping it made them feel victorious.

On the inside, I was too exhausted to feel the full extent of the joy. My endurance event of studying hard and stressing hard had taken its toll.

I had already begun to evaluate everything that I had noticed about fear, and now I was evaluating its relationship to happiness. Why should we be afraid to feel the full extent of our success and joy? Why should the fear of failure drive us so hard?

I reflected deeply about both fear and happiness. I realised that fear is an inevitable part of life. You can't just shake it off, ignore it or run away from it because it will only come back and haunt or challenge you. Much like you can't ignore a toothache by pretending it doesn't exist, the pain will only get worse.

For me, I was tired of trying to fight fear off with all my might (and alone) every time I encountered a challenge or problem in life. I was too exhausted to enjoy my wins and needed time to recover. But through all this reflection and questioning, something incredible happened. I figured out an alternative way to deal with fear in life without diminishing my happiness. I figured out a way we could all be both courageous and victorious.

I invented a system to **S.T.E.P on Fear**.

Not just once, but each and every time it rears its ugly head.

Instead of feeling overwhelmed and letting fear step on me, I decided to put any and all fear under my feet and step on it. I figured out an innovative system that works for anyone experiencing fear in life and wanting to overcome it.

I realised that getting rid of fear was almost impossible but learning how to process it and overcome it means that it can't have power over you. It can't wreck your dreams or derail your efforts. I also discovered that the most beautiful things in life can be achieved when you find what is on the other side of fear.

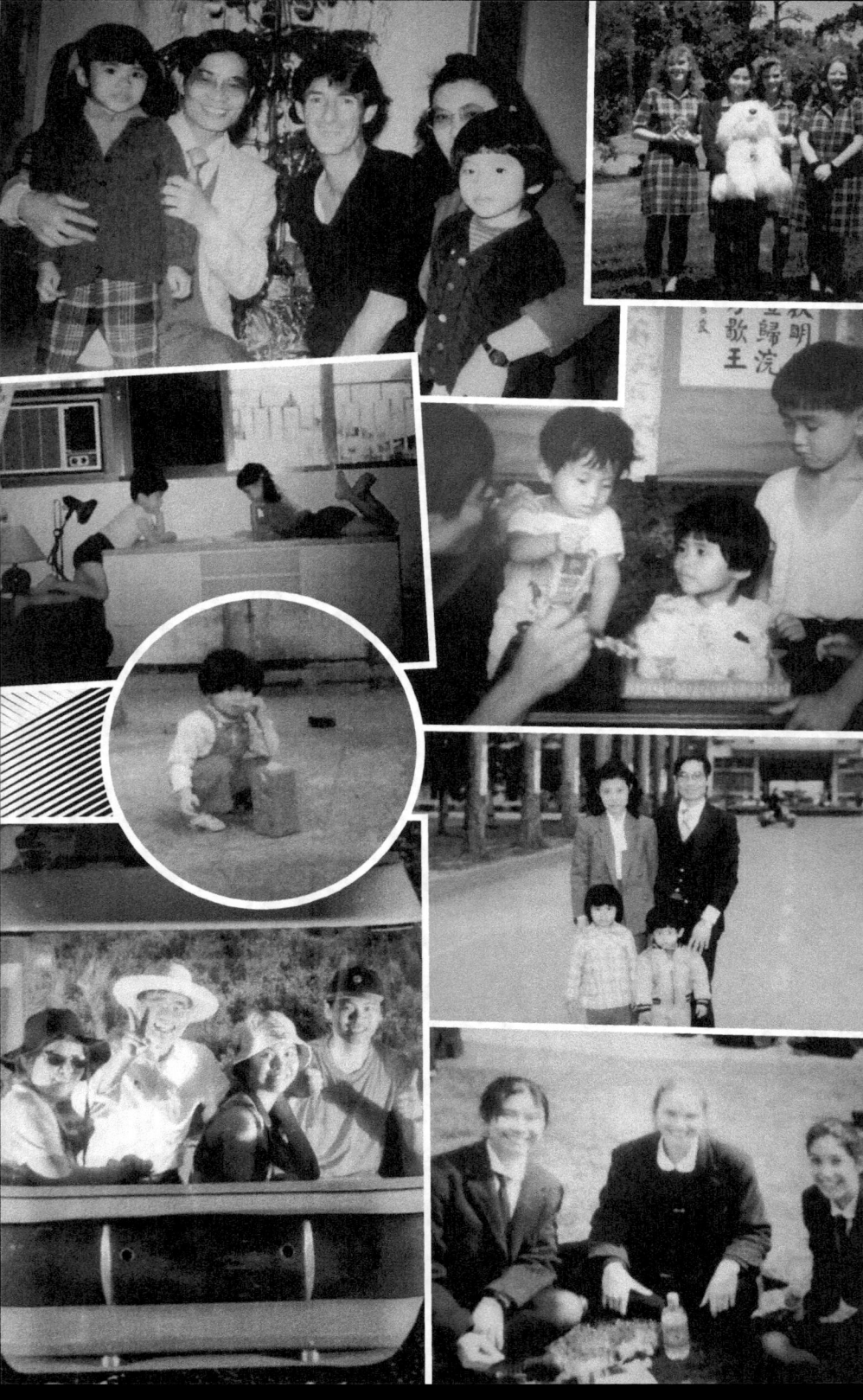

PART TWO

THE OTHER SIDE OF FEAR

> Fear has its use,
> but cowardice
> has none.
>
> **GANDHI**

CRACKING THE FEAR CODE

As you may have guessed, I became a dentist. I still am a dentist and it still fills me with absolute pride and joy. We have a wonderful clinic in Sydney and my life is dedicated to helping others, not only to give them a beautiful smile but also to help them overcome fear.

I can honestly say that without discovering my **S.T.E.P on Fear** technique, I would not have conquered the multitude of fears that naturally arise through life. No one is immune to fear, and fears don't stop when we reach our goal.

We are wired with an inbuilt fear mechanism called our fight-or-flight response, which is designed to signal fear to us in order to protect us. Interestingly, as many leading-edge psychologists will tell you, this fight or flight response that was inbuilt to protect us from danger back in the caveman days, is often triggered by modern-day fears too.

As we have evolved, this primitive part of our brain-body response has stayed the same. And today, we have a lot of new and different fears that we didn't have in ancient times. For many people that I have talked to and worked with, it's often their fears that prevent them from living their best lives.

For too long, we have allowed this basic survival mechanism to rule us. Although to some degree, this auto-regulation of our body works to adjust our response to fear, it is not always easy to transition from a chaotic situation to calmness. Human emotions are much more complex than animals' therefore if we allow fear to dominate our lives, this constant pressure and chronic negativity will drive our unconscious minds to continuously produce an influx of stress hormones. The flood of stress hormones throws our bodies out of balance and whips up a chronic state of stress that leads to further anxiety, worry and even burnout.

I am here to change that. I believe that on the other side of fear is your greatest life. You do not need to be ruled by fear.

FEAR IS NOT NOTHING

Many young kids are afraid of the dark. They are afraid that there might be monsters or goblins or something dark and nasty lurking under their bed or in their cupboard. Some kids may watch a movie or read a book and it scares them. They worry that there might be something chasing them or they might be left alone in the dark.

I remember once as a child I must have had a nightmare and was afraid that there was something in my room. I called my dad and told him that I was scared. And he said what most parents would say, "There is nothing there. There is nothing to be afraid of."

Parents may open the blinds, turn on the lights or check under the bed to reassure their child that there truly is *nothing* there. But there is something there! Fear is there. Just because something doesn't actually exist as a substance, or as an object, doesn't mean that 'nothing' is there. Some might say it is just in your mind or that it is a figment of your imagination. However there is something there and that thing is *fear*.

Know that fear *can* be stopped. Fear can be silenced. Fear doesn't need to rule your life.

It's become quite the fad to define fear as, **F**alse-**E**vidence-**A**ppearing-**R**eal. I don't buy into that. If you allow fear, worry, problems, challenges and concerns to step all over you then you can still feel overwhelmed regardless of how others try to convince you that it is just some False-Evidence-Appearing-Real. Though it may be technically 'false', you have already let it become real in your mind therefore it feels real to you. It intimidates your mind and causes limiting belief, self-doubt, imposter syndrome and of course, fear.

If you ignore it, it won't go away and will often return to haunt you or cause more damage with more complexity. If you try to fight it off with all your might, without a strategy and reserve of energy, you end up exhausted and burnt-out when yet another fear (or worry, problem, challenge) shows up right after the first one you're still trying to recover from.

So instead of believing **F**alse-**E**vidence-**A**ppearing-**R**eal, I believe that FEAR makes you:

Frustrated-**E**motional-**A**ngry-**R**esentful.

It depletes you of joy, happiness, hope and harmony.

THE TWO FEARS YOU ARE BORN WITH

Science shows that we are born with only two fears: the fear of falling and the fear of loud noises. They have tested newborn babies and discovered that these two fears are inbuilt. The rest we are taught or we 'inherit' from our parents, our culture or environment. If we are born with only two fears then why are we so full of fear?

Throughout our life we develop new fears and because we have never learned how to deal with fear, we accumulate a lot of unnecessary fears. It's like carrying around a big heavy suitcase all day long. We can put it down at any time but because we have become so comfortable carting our fears and anxieties around with us, we don't realise we can let go.

WE ARE BORN TO BOND

Human beings are not born to face the world alone. We don't like to be alone. We don't come into this world alone; another person (our mother) births us. We are naturally social beings and that's why we want to bond together. The entire human species has survived through the power of togetherness, forming families and tribes and communities that coexist and work together. The fear of being ostracised or not belonging is inbuilt within us from tribal times. When we feel that we have a reliable tribe, we often experience less fear.

But you don't need a blood-related tribe to feel this sense of belonging anymore. You can find it within like-minded communities, business groups and friendship circles. As you read this book, I would like you to think of all the other people reading this book. People just like you and me. People that also have fears and dreams. People who want to live their best lives and overcome their own personal challenges.

People that can relate to you and you can relate to them. Together we are a tribe of warriors who encourage each other to **S.T.E.P. on Fear.**

This is the way I'd like you to think of this book, as a bond that links you to other individuals who are also learning to **S.T.E.P on Fear.**

FEAR, PAIN AND SUFFERING

Have you ever stopped to ask why there is so much fear, pain, suffering and struggle in life? I have often wondered this. In fact it's been a burning question of mine since I was young. I have come to understand that fear is an inevitable part of life. If you don't know how to handle fear or how to deal with it effectively, it will result in pain.

This pain can be acute immediate pain, chronic pain or even deep pain. And if you don't know how to resolve your problem, pain can then linger on and cause further suffering. It can become a downward spiral into long suffering.

It's like a toothache. You can only treat the root cause of it. Numbing the pain with medication may provide temporary relief but it doesn't remove the cause of the problem. Ignoring it won't work either, it will remind you it's still there by heightening the pain the more you try to ignore it.

I once knew a man in his 60s who had a major fear of flying. Of course, this is a legitimate fear. He was very mechanically minded and didn't trust the mechanical engineers of the aeroplanes. He was petrified of the plane failing mid-air. He didn't investigate his fear; he simply allowed it to be his 'normal'.

At first, he could live quite happily without flying. It didn't impact his life or lead him into suffering. He never needed to fly. He worked at the local hardware store, went on local holidays or drove to his destinations. He didn't need to overcome his fear because there was no motivation for him to do so.

Until his daughter fell in love with a European man and they decided to marry overseas. He had two choices: overcome his fear of flying so he could walk his only daughter down the aisle on her wedding day, or he could keep his fear and stay home.

Sadly, the man kept his fear. He stayed stuck in the belief that he 'couldn't fly' despite the fact he had never tried to overcome his fear. He didn't take a course or talk to an expert or read a book that could help him.

By listening to his fear he missed walking his beloved daughter down the aisle and he regretted it for the rest of his life. This is just a small window of what fear can do. It can make you believe in your limitations. It can prevent you from having fun and enjoying your life.

The sad and scary part about suffering is that it doesn't just stay with that one person. Suffering can affect many others and even carry on for generations. This man's fear of flying for example affected his daughter's wedding day and her memories of it. It wasn't his fault in many ways; it was that he believed his fear. He didn't try to **S.T.E.P** on it. He believed he was incapable of living life on the other side of fear.

Fear can run like a disease and infect an entire lineage of people, even between nations. When you allow your pain to bury deeper and longer, it can be carried on and over to other people. Your pain can affect your family, friends, people around you; and theirs can affect you too. Your pain can move from your personal life to your work life or from your work life to your home life. A toxic boss can affect many workers in one day. A fearful father or mother can create anxiety within their family. Pain and suffering can transition from one generation to another; from one issue to another, from one place to everywhere, from one nation, race or culture to many.

INTERGENERATIONAL FEAR

Fear is not only personal. It doesn't just happen to one person in isolation. Sometimes fear can spread through entire cultures and infect thousands. For example, certain people may have a fear or a bad impression against another nation or culture. Not because those people harmed or attacked them directly, but they could be the descendants of a generation where a sad, hurtful incident happened in the past. These mass collective fears can trigger fighting, conflict and wars.

One of the longest running conflicts in the world between Palestine and Israel is one such example. Young children born into this conflict are taught to hate 'the enemy'. As 20th century writer and political activist Bertrand Russell says, 'Collective fear stimulates herd instinct, and tends to produce ferocity toward those who are not regarded as members of the herd.'[1]

Yet this type of intergenerational fear and fighting has significant consequences, often for the innocent. Psychologists now refer to this as 'intergenerational trauma'. It was first recognised in 1966, when psychologists noticed huge numbers of children born to Holocaust survivors began to seek professional help from clinics in Canada.

Furthermore, the number of grandchildren of the original Holocaust survivors seeking professional help was a whopping 300% higher in comparison to the general population.[2] Since then intergenerational trauma has been recognised and

---

1 Russell, Bertrand. *Unpopular Essays*. (1950), George Allen & Unwin, London.
2 Fossion P, Rejas MC, Servais L, Pelc I, Hirsch S (2003). "Family approach with grandchildren of Holocaust survivors". *American Journal of Psychotherapy*. 57 (4): 51927. doi:10.1176/appi.psychotherapy.2003.57.4.519. PMID 14735877.

observed in many groups of people including descendants of slavery, Indigenous Australians, Native Americans, Cambodian refugees and many more. Fear carries over from one generation to the next. As you can imagine, long-term intergenerational suffering will not improve our world. We must become aware of it and this is the first step to changing it.

Many of humanity's conflicts can be changed, dealt with or handled in a much better way. We can improve the emotional environment in which we raise our children and also create a culture in which brings forth the goodness within people. We can tell new stories and create new beginnings. This is not to say that we don't acknowledge the hurts of yesterday — fear, pain and suffering are all interrelated and we cannot ignore them. We must enlighten our minds and become conscious of the impact fear, pain and suffering has on people. This can happen at the **community level, a national level and international level**. We can seek to change the fear and trauma so it doesn't ripple out and wreak further havoc.

COMMUNITIES AND COUNTRIES' FEARS

Communities and countries often draw invisible boundaries between groups of people and form an 'us' versus 'them' mentality. Such boundaries are not real until you make them so in your mind.

Research conducted by Pew Research Centre in 2014 looked at fear (threats) and how they differed from country to country. The research included 44 countries and 48,643 people.[3] When asked about the greatest threats that existed

---

3 Pew Research Center. "Greatest Dangers in the World". Washington, D.C. (October 16, 2014). https://www.pewresearch.org/global/2014/10/16/greatest-dangers-in-the-world.

in the world, many countries listed experiences that had impacted them or threatened their region or country.

Most Europeans and Americans listed inequality as their greatest threat, the gap between the rich and poor being a major concern. The Middle Eastern population said that religious and ethnic hatred was their greatest threat in the world. 49% of the Japanese population cited a nuclear attack or the spread of nuclear weapons as the world's greatest threat. Africa listed infectious diseases and various Asian countries noted environmental issues among the top threats.

As you can see from this report, every region carries it's own major fears and these can vastly impact the happiness of a nation.

In today's world, it is often not fierce competition that puts people off trying to live their best lives, but the encountered inequalities and fears that leave people in a state of hopeless despair. Although we are unique individuals who are special in our own ways, we all want to be treated equally and have equal opportunities to be our best.

We must be able to equip ourselves for the journey of learning, gaining skills and knowledge for a better life, a better future, and a better world. And some of this knowledge is about *unlearning our fears*.

By empowering all and promoting inclusion and equal opportunity, we can meet the different needs of individuals and countries and provide equal access to freedom and unlimited opportunities.

FAMILY AND RELATIONAL FEAR

We can also carry fear from our families or close relationships. According to the Boston Children's Hospital – anxiety, fear, and phobias can be inherited.[4] Children can quickly develop and learn fears. But as American psychiatrist Karl Augustus Menninger said, "Fears are educated into us, and can, if we wish, be educated out."

I also believe this to be true. We don't have to follow family traditions if they disempower us. My family chose a different religion than their parents and ancestors, and though there was some anxiety and concern around this, they followed their heart and had to break family tradition in order to be true to themselves.

Many fears are born from an individual wanting to spread their own wings and some of the greatest opposition can come from our closest relatives and family members. The fear of being ostracised or kicked out of a bonded tribe can be the toughest of all fears.

Many people carry 'family fears' and have formed beliefs given to them by their parents or relatives. Growing up in an Asian culture for example, a lot of emphasis is placed on education and schooling. A child can quickly develop a fear of not pleasing their parents, or letting their parents down if they don't achieve good grades. Although my parents never once said to me, "If you don't get good grades you will dishonour the family," in my cultural upbringing and the harsh schooling system, this was the silent story running through so many young minds.

---

4 Boston Children's Hospital. "Phobias, Symptoms and Causes". Retrieved online 2nd Sept 2020. http://www.childrenshospital.org/conditions-and-treatments/conditions/p/phobias/symptoms-and-causes

INDIVIDUAL FEAR

> *"He who is not everyday conquering some fear has not learned the secret of life."*
> **— Ralph Waldo Emerson —**

Then we have our personal fears that only we can feel or are unique to our situation. Some people are scared of:
- Failing
- Losing money
- Success
- Flying or confined spaces
- Animals

The list of fears is long and fascinating. Some people have more unusual fears like a fear of clowns or balloons popping. But life is about conquering these fears, no matter how big or small. No matter how frightening or absurd, no fear feels small. All fear feels big to the person that feels it.

It is important to know that throughout our entire human history, people have had to learn how to conquer fear. We all have this in common. But often it can be hard to know where the fear started. Can you differentiate between your fear and your parents' fears? Or cultural fears imbedded into your psyche?

The important thing to know is that regardless of the origin or circumstance, all fear can be dealt with the same way. You can overcome them all.

THE COMPROMISED ZONE

The truth about staying in your comfort zone is that it is not comfortable at all. In fact, I like to call it a 'Compromised Zone', which limits your growth and restrains your potential. Of course, there will be bumps on the path from where you are to where you want to be. And sometimes you'll be happy to stay in your comfort zone, but living life inside your comfort zone is not a comfortable place to always dwell.

When people spend too much time in their comfort zone they often feel lethargic, dull and a lack of spark and purpose. It compromises you from stretching yourself further and developing a mindset that is keen to explore new horizons and opportunities, even those less familiar.

FEAR IS ABOUT MOVING FORWARD

> *"The cave you fear to enter holds
> the treasure you seek."*
> — Joseph Campbell —

I remember the day I became a citizen of Australia. We had previously been classified as immigrants for a number of years and we were very excited to receive the honour of being a national citizen. During the process, we needed to learn about the history of Australia and lots of cultural facts about being an Australian.

One of the questions they asked was, "Why did Australia choose the symbol of a kangaroo and emu in the Commonwealth Coat of Arms?" The reason was because both the emu and kangaroo cannot easily move backwards, they always move forwards. I immediately loved the spirit of that emblem. I thought, *What a beautiful spirit of Australians.* And that became a part of the driving force for me. The spirit to understand a situation is important but so is moving forward, not backwards.

Conquering fear propels you forward. That's why **Step 1** in my fear model is all about taking that step forward, towards a brighter future (more on that in the next chapter).

THE BLAME GAME

Before you decide to **S.T.E.P on Fear**, you need to give up the blame game. Blaming other people, blaming other countries or cultures, blaming family or friends that may have done you wrong. It's important to acknowledge and accept some things that may have caused you harm or concern, but also understand that giving all your energy to them prevents you from moving forward.

If you made a mistake or a serious blunder, so what? Just own it and do something about it. Don't just fall into the apology trap. If you have done something wrong and then say, "I'm sorry," that helps a little but it doesn't show anything more than you can say two little words.

It's better to say, "I'm sorry to upset you in this way. I really want to do something about it. What can I do to make it better from here?" Make a commitment to reducing the other person's pain. As the old adage goes, actions speak louder than words. As soon as you actually recognise the mistake and tell the person that you want to do something about it, you can move forward with positive action. Of course, you can only help a person when they want to be helped but it allows you to move forward with honesty and courage.

If you keep picking at an old wound it won't heal. If you let it heal you may be left with a scar to remind you of the pain but it doesn't hurt anymore. Scars have a long history in society. In ancient times, some scars symbolised an initiation into manhood or womanhood. Some were horrible (in terms of punishment for a crime) but there were many scars that were worn with pride because they had been earned. They symbolised the overcoming of a great battle or a very hard time. The hard times weren't forgotten rather they were respected.

Warriors take the lesson and feel proud to have the scar proving they made it through. They learn from the risk. Nobody says that it is easy to bear. The pain is true and the experience is true. The pain is not forgotten, it's just taken as a lesson, as a battle that was overcome.

My parents sold everything they owned in Taiwan in order to move to Australia in the business immigration stream and we were so excited to build our new Australian dream.

However the language barrier and cultural differences affected almost every aspect of our new life in Australia.

Even though Dad and Mum always said to my brother and me, "It's so nice to live in Sydney, isn't it? Such a beautiful country with so many nice people," I knew they were not happy behind their smiling faces. I struggled at school because I couldn't understand and couldn't fit in. Initially, I wanted to complain and blame others for our difficult circumstances and hardships.

Smiling through this depression made me fear more and slipped me into a downward spiral. One night I saw my parents struggling to read some school paperwork, flipping through the dictionary under the dim light, trying to make sense of the words and sentences. In the end, they could only figure out the amount they had to pay because of the numbers yet they couldn't fully understand what they were paying for. At that time, I realised that the world was bigger than my comfort zone and it was time for me to grow up and learn new things in order to become independent and to give back. The first thing I had to stop was blaming others for life's challenges.

THE LONG VIEW — EVERYTHING WILL BE OKAY

No matter what circumstances people find themselves in I often find myself saying to them, "Everything is going to be okay." Most people just laugh back sarcastically.

Then I say, "Remember this: everything is going to be okay. When it's not okay, it's not the end. So everything is going to be okay in the end. When it's not okay, it's not the end."

Yes, I crack a joke. Laughter is the best medicine. To actually help the person, it's good to laugh, or even squeeze a smile. You've got to start somewhere.

Most people need to know three things:
1. Everything will be okay in the end
2. They are not alone
3. Fear can be overcome

Many people tend to put a lot of weight on their shoulders. It's okay to be vulnerable. So many people have already gone through a similar experience, or are going through one right now, or will experience one in the future.

Australia's Health Report[5] suggests that around 4 million (one in five) Australians experience a mental illness every year. Plus around 45% of Australians aged 16–85 will experience a mental illness in their lifetime. Another report estimates that depression costs Australian businesses around $12.6 billion a year.[6]

It's important to know that you're not alone. Sometimes you can't deal with it by yourself and that's why you need a person or a group or a community — to know that you're not alone.

Early during the coronavirus pandemic of 2020, I visited my local petrol station café. It was the first Monday after a lot of small businesses were ordered to close down suddenly so it was a very scary time for a lot of people. There were many people feeling panicked and felt like they were losing direction. Some people needed to use blame — blaming other countries, the government or even people around them.

---

5 Australian Institute of Health and Welfare 2018. Australia's health 2018. Australia's health series no. 16. AUS 221. Canberra: AIHW. https://www.aihw.gov.au/getmedia/7c42913d-295f-4bc9-9c24-4e44eff4a04a/aihw-aus-221.pdf)

6 LaMontagne AD, Sanderson K, & Cocker F (2010): Estimating the economic benefits of eliminating job strain as a risk factor for depression: summary report. Victorian Heath Promotion Foundation (VicHealth), Melbourne, Australia. https://www.vichealth.vic.gov.au/~/media/ResourceCentre/PublicationsandResources/Economic%20participation/Job%20strain/P-022-SC_Job_Strain_SUMMARY_October2010_V12.ashx)

It was a very gloomy day for many. On this particular Monday morning, the miserable weather reflected the mood. So when I visited the shop to get my usual coffee, there was a staff member I often saw there called Warren. Warren is a very nice guy, always very funny and smiling. But this particular morning he looked very disturbed and worried. I could see his troubled mind. I wanted to cheer him up so I said, "Hey Warren, I'd love my usual large flat white, how is your day?"

Warren said, "Okay, large, flat white."

I could tell he was curious as to why I was so happy and smiling. I said, "By the way, I really, really like your coffee, because it always brightens my day. It's such a good way to start the day."

He managed a tiny smile in response. I thanked him for my coffee and gave him the biggest smile possible. The next customer asked for a bag of ice and Warren had to go outside to the ice chest. Warren looked up to the sky as the rain drizzled on his face. I overheard him say, "God, where is the sun?"

In many ways, it was the ultimate metaphor for life. Lockdown had just begun and people were losing their jobs. I turned to Warren and said, "Don't worry, the sun will come."

As I walked back to my car, I remembered this glorious song called, 'Sun Above The Clouds' by Stream of Praise. It was originally written in Mandarin but I love to add my own words to any catchy tune, so I did my own translation and had a little singsong in the car with my coffee.

That afternoon it turned out to be a sunny day with beautiful blue skies and white wispy clouds. It made me think of Warren and I hoped he had noticed the sunshine.

The next day, I returned to the shop to get my usual coffee. Due to the new protocols there was now a protective screen between Warren and the customers. I said, "Hey Warren, the sun has come out!" I could see him smiling from behind the screen. Despite the physical distancing protocols, the bonding of smiling breaks that invisible barrier instantly.

The next morning when I went to get my coffee, Warren was joking behind the clear screen. He said, "Cathy, you need to cheer me up more. Every time you come in, I'm not cheerful enough, you bring it out more."

It only took a week to see Warren go from doom and gloom to smiling like the sky above the clouds. That's because tough times don't last, tough people do. And I don't mean tough as in muscles and brawn, I mean resilience. Resilient people outlast tough times.

It's important for people to know that they are not alone in their troubles. True happiness is all about having people around you to be happy with you, not just by you or for you. When I was a child, I used to think my happiest moment was when I felt my parents were happy but I came to understand that happiness is always better shared.

You don't just want to be happy. You don't want people to be happy for you. You want people to be happy together, *with* you.

I was happy the morning I entered that petrol station café for my coffee, but I didn't just want to have all the happiness for myself. I wanted to see Warren happy and other people happy, so we could all enjoy it together. As the great Maya Angelou said, "People will forget what you said, people will forget what you did, but people will never forget how you made them feel."[7]

---

7 Angelou, M., 2016. *Caged Bird Legacy | The Legacy Of Dr. Maya Angelou*. [online] Retrieved 14 March 2016. http://www.mayaangelou.com

> "The Lord is my light and my salvation; whom shall I fear?
>
> The Lord is the stronghold of my life; of whom shall I be afraid?"
>
> **PSALM 27:1,
> THE BIBLE (NIV)**

THE PROCESS OF PAIN

Pain usually gets all negative attention but sometimes pain has positives too. Pain is just part of life's process. We all have a certain amount of pain that we will endure.

A caterpillar has to go alone into the darkness of a chrysalis in order to grow wings and transform into a beautiful butterfly. Is it painful to break through the chrysalis? It certainly looks challenging.

But if you try to help the butterfly by breaking the chrysalis for it, you may actually prevent it from flying or even living. In fact, the butterfly needs the struggle to survive. As it pushes its fragile body out of the chrysalis, fluid gets pushed into its body and wings helping it to fly. If the butterfly is denied the struggle, it doesn't get strong enough to fly and often dies.

As a human species, we are lucky in the fact that we do have people that can help us. But if you feel alone in the struggle, perhaps you are just growing your wings. Maybe you are ready to fly very soon? Remember it always seems darkest just before the dawn.

When I gave birth to my first child Sarah, I had never experienced that kind of pain in my entire life. The pain came so quick, so fast, so intense, I had no time to even consider asking for pain relief. It was a natural birth and I literally felt that I could die. Of course, the pain is most unbearable right before the baby arrives. The painful contractions are in fact pushing your beautiful baby out into the light.

I remember talking to myself in a way that I had never spoken to myself before. I said, *It's okay, even if I die, as long as the baby is safe and healthy.* To be honest, I never thought like that before I became a mum. The pain birthed a new inner resource inside of me. Many mothers will agree that as you surrender your body to the excruciating pain, the unconditional love inside of you is at its highest peak.

Now because my first childbirth was quite traumatic, I didn't know how I would cope the second time around. But I knew one thing; that there would be pain. I needed to focus on something greater than the pain. So I focused on the birth of the baby and kept telling myself that the pain's job was to push my baby to me. I had a great medical team and I kept reminding myself of all their experience. When he arrived I kept telling him, "I love you. I love you. I love you." I didn't get to experience that joy with my first labour because I was too scared about the fine line between life and death.

Sometimes without the pain we don't appreciate the beauty.

I met a wonderful man, Khoa Nam Tran at the Speakers Institute in Sydney. We were speaking at the same special event. Khoa lost both of his legs in a car accident and now walks on metal rods. He said that the accident allowed him to become 'more' of himself; it gave him new resources within, giving him a deeper sense of gratitude and appreciation for life.

Pain has a transformational ability hidden inside. We just need to look for the lessons.

LEARN AT ANY AND ALL STAGES

When you feel that you can learn at every stage in life and from any experience, fear begins to automatically reduce. Have you ever had to give a talk on stage? There can be a tug-of-war between fear and excitement. Part of you is scared to talk in public and the other part is excited to share your message.

So in any situation you can feel the fear and the excitement because something amazing is there waiting for you to discover, waiting for you to really take that first step. Then when you take that step you move from fear to excitement. Quite often you forget about the negative, narrow-minded side that fear presented because you're having too much fun. You transitioned away from fear just by taking one tiny step. Over time, all these little steps become your stepping-stones. Without them, how are you going to reach from point A to point B?

> *"The world we see that seems so insane is the result of a belief system that is not working. To perceive the world differently, we must be willing to change our belief system, let the past slip away, expand our sense of now, and dissolve the fear in our minds."*

> *"To feel brave, act as if we were brave, use all our will to that end, and courage will very likely replace fear."*
> — William James —

THE LESSONS WE GAIN THROUGH PAIN

Pain will go away. But it is important for us to remember the lessons we gained. Some people say short-term pain, long-term gain. Not all experiences will be life lessons but some of the most challenging ones will be. If you don't treasure it, you don't remember it. If it doesn't challenge you, you don't take in the feedback or learn from it.

We don't just remember days, weeks, months, years, we remember the moments. And we remember the people who helped and/or hurt us in those moments. That's why it's important to actively seek the lessons you learned and the qualities you used. Lao Tzu said, "New beginnings are often disguised as painful endings." That's why it's always important to remember that you are not alone in your troubles.

When Mother Teresa saw people suffering every day, she realised the greatest suffering in the world is loneliness. She spent her whole life helping people, particularly the poor and sick in the slums in India. I remember one documentary where she was cradling a man who was dying. Mother Teresa held him in her arms. The journalist asked her, "Even though you know he is going to die, why do you do this?"

The person passed away with a smile on his face as he whispered to Mother Teresa, "Thank you for being here." I think that moment answered the journalist's question, don't you?

Her legacy still lives on. And so do many others. By passing on your own legacy, you can reduce suffering and add more beauty to the world. A lot of people are searching for high positions in life or society. You actually don't need much to live on. What is most important is your purpose in life because your legacy lives on when you leave this world.

Monarch butterflies can take four generations to migrate, each generation flies as far as possible until they die and the next generation takes over. They don't know necessarily why they are flying but in the end all generations' efforts end up making a super generation of Monarchs to continue their species.

We are very much the same. Often, we don't know why we are pushing new limits or going that extra mile but quite often we are leaving a legacy behind. We are trail blazing new territory for the next generation.

Catherine is sharing more in her INTERACTIVE book.

See exclusive behind-the-scenes videos, audios and photos.

DOWNLOAD it now at
deanpublishing.com/steponfear

> Although the world is
> full of suffering,
> it is full also of the
> overcoming of it.
>
> **HELEN KELLER**

BE FAITHFUL TO THE SMALL

That is why you need to learn how to **S.T.E.P. on Fear** so that you can be who you want to be, do what you want to do and live how you want to live. All great journeys start with something small, and you need to learn to be faithful to the small.

> A journey of a thousand miles begins with a single step
> 千里之行, 始於足下

I would like to give you an example of being faithful to the small. I belong to a wonderful initiative called B1G1 (B1G1.com) often classified as a conscious 'Business for Good'. Its basic premise is Buy1Give1. The founder Masami Sato is an advocate for the power of small and in 2007, she started B1G1 with a simple idea: What if every business could make a difference in their own way, just by doing what they normally do?

More than a decade later, this simple idea became a global movement. When businesses deliver their normal service or product, a portion of each transaction goes to a charity and becomes an impact. An impact can mean clean water to an impoverished community, seeds to a poor farming family, business loans to a single working mother, and so much more. It's a truly magnificent way for all small businesses to make a difference without breaking their bank account.

Here are some examples of how a small business can help: every time a client accepts a cup of tea or coffee at reception, we provide one day's worth of grain to nourish a child in Malawi. Every time a new patient appointment is made, we provide one daily dose of vitamin A supplements to a child in Turkana, Kenya. When we see a client for emergency care, we plant a tree to support reforestation in Borneo.

When we provide painless dentistry using IV sedation, we give a meal to a rescued animal through Edgar's Mission in Victoria, Australia. When a new child sits in the dental chair, happily counting teeth with us, we provide one day of education support to a disadvantaged child in New Zealand. When a client laughs in the dental chair and thanks us for an enjoyable dental experience, we provide one day of access to personal hygiene to a girl in Kenya or Nepal.

When a client returns for their six-month dental check-up, we provide one day of access to dental hygiene to a child in El Jebha, Morocco. When a client's smile is transformed by functional aesthetics, four rainforest trees are planted and protected to help the survival of the southern cassowary at Mission Beach in Queensland, Australia.

When we perform the Chats Dental Puppet Show to educate pre-schoolers and schoolchildren, we give one special learning tool to a child in Buffalo City, South Africa. When we give out a 'Certificate of Gratitude' to a valued client, we give one day of access to reading materials to a girl in Cambodia.

So after I joined B1G1, I brought that giving concept to our dental practice. I said to our team, "Okay, from now on, we're going to offer every client a drink and each time someone accepts the drink, I want you to record it so we can calculate the drinks and then help our new charity projects." Everyone thought that was a great idea, so we implemented it.

Initially, we did it all wrong. When we asked a client, we would say, "Would you like a drink of water?" They would say, "No, thank you." As you may have guessed, we weren't giving much in the first week or two.

I decided to talk to our team and show them some more encouraging techniques. I asked some of our team to change the way they asked the question. "Perhaps you could say, 'Mr Phillips, it's such a hot day outside, may I offer you a glass of cool water while you're waiting for the doctor to be ready?'"

I could tell the team where thinking, *Yeah, right Catherine'* But I persisted, "Just trust my words. Use your heart and pick the right moment." We did a little rehearsal and brought in some new types of tea and coffee to offer.

When Mr Phillips arrived, he was running late and came in panting and couldn't catch his breath. Our lovely team member greeted him nicely and said, "May I please make a cup of tea for you Mr Phillips? I'd love you to relax and take some time for yourself."

"But I'm going to have my teeth cleaned." He was worried it may stain his teeth.

As we had rehearsed, our team member replied, "That's absolutely fine. You are most welcome to enjoy a cup of tea because Catherine is going to clean your teeth later anyway."

He instantly relaxed and took a cup of lemon ginger tea handed to him with a smile, "Mr Phillips, please enjoy. Take your time, it's all fine."

Halfway through his cup of tea he said, "Thank you, I feel so much better. I'm ready now."

When I saw him, I said, "Hello Mr Phillips, thank you so much for coming. How are you today?"

He replied, "Honestly Catherine, I don't know what you guys put into that cup of tea but I was feeling so stressed today and now I feel so much better. I can't believe that I am actually looking forward to coming to the dentist."

That is a true story. It shows how taking care of the small details is really taking care of the big details. Being faithful to the small can alter the big. The famous poet Emily Dickinson said, "If you take care of the small things, the big things take care of themselves. You can gain more control over your life by paying closer attention to the little things."

I believe this is true. You don't need to be a superhero to overcome fear; you just need to do the small things well.

Stanford University behavioural scientist, BJ Fogg found out how doing the smallest habit changed his view of human behaviour.[8] Suffering from despair over the tragic loss of his nephew and an impending business failure, he couldn't sleep properly for weeks.

One morning, after a particularly restless night he saw himself in the mirror and wondered if this was the day that the wheels would finally fall off. He picked up the dental floss but this only added to his despair; he'd never been able to get into a regular habit of flossing his teeth.

He decided that instead of trying to floss all his teeth and failing again, he would just floss one. That way if the entire day went wrong, at least he wouldn't be a total failure — he had flossed one tooth.

After he flossed that solitary tooth he said, "Victory!"

But the fascinating thing about this story is that as a behavioural scientist, he had stumbled on something groundbreaking. He applied his simple method to other things he wanted to conquer and he saw how the power of very tiny habits can in fact alter our entire lives. How just doing one step with minimal motivation required, propels us into new and positive habits because they are so easy to do. Yes, even flossing one tooth can be the beginning of a new and positive relationship.

---

8   https://www.tinyhabits.com/about

> Not all of us can do great things. But we can do small things with great love.
>
> **MOTHER TERESA**

YOUR NEXT STEP

In the next chapter we are going to take that first tiny step.

You are going to learn about stepping on fear so that fear is beneath you rather than above you pushing you down and stopping you from living your dreams.

Being faithful to the small things means that we will learn new powerful skills when the stakes are low. Then we can practise how to be true and loyal to our small endeavours and behaviours in order to do the same when the stakes (or fear) are much higher.

Here is my **Straight-A-Model** that can help you use obstacles as stepping-stones. These are the small lessons that have made a big difference in my life.

ACKNOWLEDGE AND ACCEPT

- See your obstacle as a great learning
- Look for the lessons inside the challenge
- Acknowledge your fears — intergenerational/national/family/individual
- Remember pain can be purposeful
- Wear your scars with pride.

APOLOGISE AND ASK FOR THE ANSWERS

- When you make a mistake, own it and apologise
- Ask quality questions
- Listen for the answers
- Stop the blame game
- Actions speak louder than words.

ADVICE, APPRECIATION AND ACTION
- Ask for help and advice
- Show your appreciation for it
- Take immediate action
- You are not alone — the sun is just above the clouds.

ADVANCE AND ACHIEVE
- Once you establish a solid foundation, keep advancing forward
- Achieve higher with each step like the emu and kangaroo method
- It will always be okay in the end
- Move out of your Compromised Zone
- Take one small step.

PART THREE

S.T.E.P. On Fear

> The greatest glory
> in living lies not in
> never falling,
> but in rising
> every time we fall.
>
> **NELSON MANDELA**

TAKING YOUR FIRST STEP

As you know English is my second language, so I love to keep things simple. It's easier to understand, to apply and be persistent with. I remember one of my mentors told me, "You'll lose people if you say something longer than four words." He insisted on the 'keep-it-simple method.'

So I began to think of the easiest way to communicate my message about fear and one's ability to deal with it. I have encountered all sorts of challenges, hardships and problems just like everybody else, but I wanted a method that suited all situations that anyone could use. An approach that didn't require a college degree to figure out and wasn't too complicated to put into use.

It is often said that the first step is the hardest, but we shouldn't forget that it's also the most important because it unlocks the next cascade of steps. As the great Martin Luther

King Jnr said, "You don't have to see the whole staircase, just take the first step."

So, I have made you a staircase through my **S.T.E.P. on Fear** method. The beauty is, you can hold my hand and do one step at a time. Remember the immortal moon landing quote that echoed through people's televisions, "One small step for man, one giant leap for mankind." This is the way my model works too. Your small step becomes a giant leap in the end. But you must take the first step to begin!

A MODEL THAT WORKS

We humans have a deeply curious nature. Curiosity is a basic element of our cognition. By seeking information about our environment, we learn to navigate it. When we explore and satisfy our curiosity the brain releases a neurohormone called Dopamine.

Together, Dopamine, Oxytocin, Serotonin and Endorphins (D.O.S.E.) are the quartet of neurotransmitter chemicals responsible for making us feel happy. When our curiosity is suppressed or left searching in vain, we feel lost. Being lost is not just a location, it is a failure of the mind and it often results in doubt, disbelief, grief and worry. These feelings create a sense of helplessness and can make a person feel **F**rustrated, **E**motional, **A**ngry or **R**esentful = **FEAR**.

Just as the lyrics in the beloved hymn 'Amazing Grace' by John Newton say, "I once was lost, but now am found, was blind but now I see," getting lost is not scary if you have a compass to follow to help find your way back, or even better find a way forward in life.

Throughout history and the cultures around the world, there have been many different models and ideas to help people through their fear, some work and of course many do not. Something that helped me develop my own model was realising that some people do not recognise that they are lost at first. They do not question why their heart doesn't sing, why their soul feels fear.

I learnt that human beings like predictable patterns in their life and they usually prefer to follow the trend and stay in a comfort zone (or 'compromised zone' if you remember from Part 2). Some people can frankly acknowledge this behaviour of themselves but many people are not aware how much their own thoughts and actions are influenced by the patterns and trends they see in the people around them, in their cultural patterns. They do not question them.

It made me understand that sometimes people are unable to help themselves to look up and be curious; it is deeply ingrained in them to continue on as they have for so long, even over generations. So I asked myself how could I reintroduce their curiosity, inject them with positivity for life to help pinpoint what the problem is, what is actually disturbing their heart and soul and causing their fear, and help them understand how it is affecting their life. The answer is my **S.T.E.P. on Fear** model that breaks down their barriers and reignites their curiosity.

My model guides you like a compass in a four-step-process that is easy to understand and simple to follow. You can rely on this model to guide you through the processes that change fears into cheers!

THE FEAR FACTOR

To some people the word *fear* might not seem a very nice word, it can conjure up some negative connotations; they might not want to talk about it or they get scared just at the mention of the word. It can cause people's imaginations to run away and their body to shudder.

Other people may relate the word fear to something exciting, like skydiving or extreme sports. Others use fear for motivation and drive, for example, fear of becoming overweight may ignite someone to start exercising, or fear of losing one's money might inspire them to open a trust account.

For me, the word fear is all about transformation: utilising your fear in a way that propels you forward. Therefore, it doesn't matter if you perceive your fear as positive or negative, either outlook can be utilised to benefit you if you know how to use it. As Eleanor Roosevelt said, "You gain strength, courage and confidence by every experience in which you really stop to look fear in the face."

You first conquer fear by looking straight at it, by sitting still and being honest about what you are feeling. Not by shying away from it.

I believe that fear is a very good word to use because it allows us to open up and have a conversation about it. You can talk about it superficially, or you can actually dig deeper. But time and time again I have noticed that looking at fear first provides the light of transformation to enter. So that's why I choose that word. Fear is like a window of possibility that people are often yet to explore.

Another reason why I believe in using fear as the opener for exploring your human potential is because it is emotional. Science shows that our emotional drivers are in fact making all of our subconscious decisions, so to ignore what is driving you (even if you think it's currently negative) could in fact be a big mistake. We can only make major changes when we become conscious of what is driving us.

Fear is a normal human emotion that everyone feels from time to time and some of the greatest and most common human fears include public speaking, confined spaces, snakes and spiders, the dentist, flying, fear of heights and especially fear of the unknown (FOTU).

Around one person in four experiences some form of anxiety disorder during their lifetime.[1] I personally expect that to rise as I am currently writing this book while the Coronavirus is most prevalent and fear is at an all-time global high. Most people I know (including myself) have never lived through a pandemic and this naturally induces new feelings of uncertainty into people's lives.

Diagnostic data from a US source, the National Comorbidity Survey Replication (NCS-R), estimated that 9.1% of adults *have a specific* phobia, while an estimated 12.5% of adults *experience a specific* phobia during their lives.[2] That's only for specific phobias; imagine the data for fear in general.

Of course, general fears are harder to measure and there's possibly no need to if we ask a rhetorical question; who hasn't experienced fear at some point during their lives? I think it's universal. Clinical psychologist Associate Professor Gavin Beccaria from the University of Southern Queensland (USQ)

---

[1] Martin, Patrick. "The epidemiology of anxiety disorders: a review." *Dialogues in clinical neuroscience* vol. 5,3 (2003): 281-98. https://www.ncbi.nlm.nih.gov/pmc/articles/PMC3181629/?xid=PS_smithsonian

[2] Harvard Medical School, 2007. National Comorbidity Survey (NCS). (2017, August 21). Retrieved from https://www.hcp.med.harvard.edu/ncs/index.php. Data Table 1: Lifetime prevalence DSM-IV/WMH-CIDI disorders by sex and cohort

said the stress that people feel about their fears was very real and needed to be acknowledged.[3]

I couldn't agree more. We must acknowledge fear of any and all sort in order to first overcome it. When fear gets in the way and limits you, it starts to clip those beautiful wings with which you are supposed to fly freely.

And here's the thing about fear, you don't even have to have some 'thing' to fear. Dr Nicholas Carleton from the Anxiety and Illness Behaviours Laboratory, Department of Psychology, at the University of Regina Canada, wrote an incredibly illuminating publication all about fear. In it Dr Carleton states that, "Fear of the unknown may be a, or possibly the, fundamental fear."[4] Even change is an unknown and a vast majority of people fear change.

As a dentist, I see and deal with people's fear every week. Fear of the unknown is something I see happening more and more (even outside the dental clinic). Fear of uncertainty can relate to a range of issues such as:

- Climate change
- Pandemics
- Relationships
- The economy
- Job security and job loss
- Health and illness
- Dying

---

[3] ABC News. Lloyd, Shelley. "Phobias of fish, spiders among 'irrational' fears for up to 15pc of population". Published online Tuesday 3 December 2019. https://www.abc.net.au/news/2019-12-03/phobias-a-risk-for-15-per-cent-of-population/11734718

[4] Carleton, R. Nicholas. (2016). Fear of the Unknown: One Fear to Rule them All?. *Journal of Anxiety Disorders*. Page 39-41. https://doi.org/10.1016/j.janxdis.2016.03.011

> The oldest and strongest emotion of mankind is fear, and the oldest and strongest kind of fear is fear of the unknown.
>
> **H.P. LOVECRAFT**

The list of unknowns goes on. Fear of the unknown is alive and thriving in today's society. But I am here to let you know that it doesn't have to control you or steer your life. There are other options than to be at the mercy of fear. You don't have to be left quivering and shaking at the thought of fear.

Research has found that after a bout of anxiety, the emotional aftermath can affect you for up to four hours. Separate research also shows that even one five-minute episode of anger can impair your immune system for more than six hours.[5]

So anxiety, anger and other emotions are having a major impact on our physical and emotional wellbeing. They are causing deeper problems. But the good news is that science has also revealed that persistently thinking about a positive event actually lengthens feelings of joy, and these warm, fuzzy feelings can last up to six hours too.[6]

This is why I believe that fear isn't just **F**alse-**E**vidence-**A**ppearing-**R**eal, but it actually makes you physically feel:

Frustrated
Emotional
Angry
Resentful

---

5   Rein G, Atkinson, M, McCraty R. "The Physiological and Psychological Effects of Compassion and Anger", *Journal of Advancement in Medicine*. 1995; 8(2): 87-105.. https://www.heartmath.org/research/research-library/basic/physiological-and-psychological-effects-of-compassion-and-anger/

6   Verduyn, P., Lavrijsen, S. "Which emotions last longest and why: The role of event importance and rumination". *Motiv Emot* 39, 119–127 (2015). https://doi.org/10.1007/s11031-014-9445-y.
https://link.springer.com/article/10.1007%2Fs11031-014-9445-y#citeas

THE FEAR TEST

Consider the following questions to see whether fear is stopping you from achieving your best:

1. Do you often worry about what other people think of you/your job/your ability?
2. Are you scared of failing or not being good enough?
3. Do you spend a lot of your day/time worrying about things that may happen that aren't in your control?
4. Do you stop yourself from doing things you love from fear of being criticised or judged?
5. Do you have secret dreams and ambitions but haven't taken action toward them?
6. Do you sabotage yourself and/or your success?
7. Do you spend a lot of time worrying about the future?

If you answered 'yes' to any of the above then fear is appearing in your life and holding you back. You don't need to hang on to this burden anymore.

Sometimes these problems or worries feel really heavy and overwhelming. I often describe it as feeling like there's a cloud raining upon you, and wherever you go that cloud follows you with its dark and threatening shadows.

The whole sky becomes really dark and you feel that you have nowhere to go because the cloud keeps following you.

But I want you to know that there is somewhere you can go and it's not to run and hide from the dark looming clouds. You must head above the clouds so you can look down on them. A place where the sun is shining and the clouds can't rain on you. There is freedom above the clouds.

Another way to describe fear is like carrying around heavy luggage everywhere you go. You just drag it around with you day and night not thinking that you can put it down. Your whole life feels like it's draining you and the fear and angst gets carted around with you everywhere.

You feel exhausted all the time and begin to complain how life is hard and tiring. If you go to the shops, for a walk, to visit friends — you take your trusty old luggage that is filled to the brim with nothing but pain, fear and suffering. You don't feel that you can put it down because it's your 'life burden' to carry.

MONDAY

When you come home, you hide it under your bed and fall asleep exhausted and overwhelmed.

Then the next morning, you pick it back up and start the heavy lifting all over again. There's so much fear and baggage to cart around that it's draining the life out of you.

TUESDAY

So instead of carrying this fear, you can learn how to put it down. Put it under your feet, and you can step on it. Raise yourself higher and use fear as a platform to get a better perspective.

I love the English word *perspective* because it means viewing something from different angles, from a different position or place, and different people can view the same thing differently. You can see the whole panorama of your life when you're higher in perspective.

THE PROBLEM HAS NO EMOTION

When you have a problem, the truth is the problem itself has no emotion. The human has the emotion; the problem is just a problem. It depends how you first look at it, and then how you perceive it, and then how you allow it to affect you or not. So if the problem doesn't change its size, it doesn't change the nature of it. If you look at a problem up close you can't see anything else because it blocks your whole view. You feel so trapped and overwhelmed. You think the problem is huge and insurmountable.

But imagine if you learn how to see the problem differently by taking a step away from it, and then learning how to step on it? All of a sudden, that huge obstacle you thought was insurmountable becomes a step-up for you to see from a higher perspective.

Imagine a 100-storey building. At ground level, if you look out of the window, you only see the ground level, right? Maybe a street, some neighbouring buildings and concrete footpaths, some people walking past. You can only see the ground level perspective.

But if you jump in the elevator and go to the penthouse right at the top, you see a completely different view. You see sky and clouds, birds and maybe an aeroplane flying past. The people below look smaller because you're up higher. You see a different and wider view of the world. Now, you didn't change, only your position and perspective did.

> "Your perspective will either become your prison or your passport."
> — Steve Furtick[7] —

Now, if you can't change your position or circumstance then you still have control in how you choose your attitude and perspective. The great psychologist and Holocaust survivor Viktor E. Frankl noticed this very thing. He noticed that the ones who gave their life meaning during the horrific time of the

---

7   Steve Furtick, Facebook, 27th October, 2015.

Holocaust gained something deeper and enduring. Frankl said, "When we are no longer able to change a situation — we are challenged to change ourselves."

THE PROBLEM GETS BIGGER IF YOU IGNORE IT

Now perspective is one thing, ignoring your problem is another.

I want to tell you about one of my clients, let's call him Sam. Sam is a physically big guy. He is in the Special Forces and looks the stereotypical guy that you'd imagine could handle anything. He's a muscle-bound tough guy and can make anyone afraid of him with one glance: until he visits me, his dentist.

One day, Sam came into the clinic with some major tooth and gum swelling. I looked at it and said, "Well Sam, this type of thing takes time to develop. You must have had this for a while?"

Sam looked smaller all of a sudden and squirmed in the dental chair. "Yeah, well...I was too scared of coming to the dentist."

Sam went on to tell me how his wife started to complain of his bad breath and wouldn't let him in their bed anymore. He kept toughing it out determined that it would one day magically disappear.

He began to drink vodka to curb the pain. Until he finally admitted to me that the, "Vodka didn't work so good anymore." After weeks, possibly months of trying to manage his sore tooth and gums, Sam finally realised that it wasn't going away, in fact, it was getting worse.

He looked so fragile in the dental chair. His declining relationship with his wife and his new drinking habit soon revealed something more sinister — that it wasn't the tooth holding him back it was fear. His fear of coming to the dentist was so strong that he nearly allowed a medical issue (his tooth), a relationship issue (his wife) and a behavioural issue (drinking vodka) to become 'normal'. These problems were in fact bigger than his fear and could have potentially sent his life into a downward spiral if he hadn't at last faced it.

I thanked him for being so brave and coming in when he needed help. I said, "You just did the most amazing thing Sam. You took the first step toward your recovery and healing and you should give yourself a big applause for that."

He didn't look convinced, nor did he believe he was brave.

I said to him, "I want to thank you because without your trust in me, I won't be able to have a look and try to help you. I think trust takes a lot of courage too."

I did everything I could during that treatment to ensure that Sam felt safe, that he knew he was in good hands and that I would take care of him. We talked honestly about his treatment plan and we focused on his health and wellbeing. I found the right moment to tell him how much I wanted him to be well and not sick and also educate him on the serious problem at hand — that if he failed to get treatment it would cause a major health concern for him.

The treatment went really well. I was focused on Sam's wellbeing — emotionally and physically. I knew Sam was scared and that he was embarrassed to be scared. Here was an enormously huge tough dude exposing his true fear. I didn't take it lightly.

Sam grew to face his fear and what began as fixing his sore and swollen tooth ended up as months of Sam's 'transformation' inside and outside. He began to look after his smile and booked in for cleaning and whitening and his check-ups too. His smile is now radiant!

A few weeks after Sam's first treatment, we received a card, not from him but from his wife. His wife wrote: *Dr Catherine and your team. I am so grateful for the way you and your team looked after my husband. I didn't know that my husband could be even better looking! Thank you for taking such great care of him.*

Now, some people may think that this is a dental transformation first and foremost but it's not. You can really change a person's heart and soul through combating fear. Remember, the problem doesn't change itself. The problem is just a problem. The person changes the problem. The proper attitude and the right treatment will go a long way.

And that is why this formula for **S.T.E.P. on Fear** has been designed. To give people the right treatment to their gnawing problems. It doesn't matter how big or small you see the problem right now, it is important for you to understand that regardless of the size, or the extensiveness of the problem, you can always step on it and then you can see over it.

You can use it to your advantage and build a great foundation. Yes, use fear as your foundation to step higher. Each separate step of the process is designed to take you steadily and carefully higher and higher, until you are above the clouds and looking down on your old fears and behaviours.

Each step is deliberately designed so you can rest on a steady platform before you take the next step. It is designed so you don't tumble back into your pre-existing condition (like the shape of a hill would be). Each step is an independent and firm 'base camp' from which you can rest and reflect until you take the next step.

The benefits of using my **S.T.E.P. on Fear** model are so you can:
- Take each step at your own pace without the risk of slipping down. Use the step-by-step process instead of going against a steep learning curve or going uphill (and against the wind).
- Take a rest at any step whenever you want to take a breath or look at the changing view. You can look back at your progress, get recharged and pumped and motivated by your achievement until you are ready to take the next step upwards.
- Feel the security as you climb. The platform of each step is wide and broad, giving you the added security and reassurance of each step.
- Take time for self-reflection and reach out in the proximity, knowing that there are supportive, like-minded people close at hand, so when you need a companion, a listening ear or a helping hand — you have a tribe.
- Visualise the possibilities. You don't need to feel daunted, overwhelmed or exhausted. You can feel in control of your life and be happy at every stage throughout the process.
- Enjoy the journey. You don't have to make it to the top or reach your destination in one go (or to make it at all). You don't need to run your race all alone or climb the uphill journey into success as a lonely winner.

My **S.T.E.P. on Fear** model works for individuals, groups, communities, and global sectors. You can use it in your personal and professional life, with your family or at school or in your work and career. It is based on the mindset of *abundance*, not scarcity. It is a framework that involves a good team to cheer you on along the journey and to celebrate with your progress and to share your vision.

So how do you do it?
S.T.E.P. on Fear is a structure with four key processes:

> **S**etting of the Mind
> **T**ools
> **E**njoyment
> **P**urpose

These processes are all connected to one another like a chain pulling you up. For each step, you must specify and clarify the content of each step before you start embarking on the next phase of your journey.

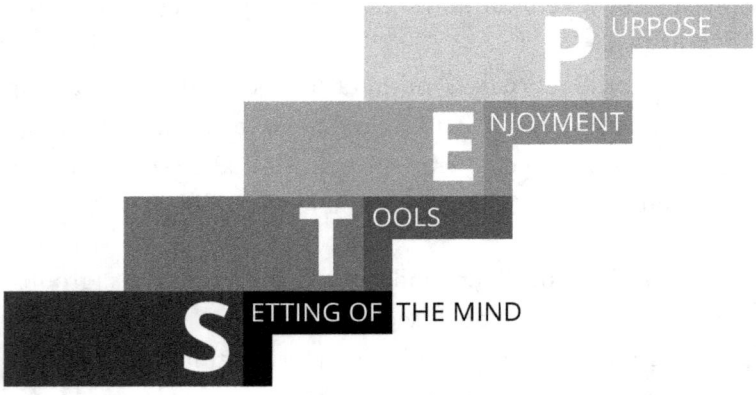

The **S.T.E.P. on Fear** model means that you can take it at your own pace, pause when you need to or revise your progress at any point in time along the journey. Sometimes you may feel like slipping back into the first step on **Setting of the Mind**, needing to shift your mindset or gain some motivation to step back on track. Sometimes you may feel the existing tools and resources are not efficient or useful enough and you may need to explore different ones by spending more time in the second stage on **Tools**.

However, you must go through all four processes without missing any one of the components in order to complete each specific step. If the journey for stepping on a specific fear is not completed properly, that unresolved fear will most likely return with more complications and more pain.

That's why it is important to step through each and every process, so you can rise like the phoenix and **S.T.E.P. on Fear** once and for all.

Catherine is sharing more in her INTERACTIVE book.

See exclusive behind-the-scenes videos, audios and photos.

DOWNLOAD it now at
deanpublishing.com/steponfear

> Always choose faith over fear.
>
> **DR CATHERINE YANG**

STEP 1
SETTING OF THE MIND

Everything starts with the mind. Lao Tzu, Margaret Thatcher, Mahatma Gandhi and many great people said a similar thing: your thoughts become your words, your words become your actions, your actions become your habits, your habits shape your character and your character designs your destiny.

Mindset is a collection of beliefs and thoughts that mould a person's mentality and attitude. Mindset influences a person's emotions and perceptions and affects a person's decisions and responses to events and circumstances.

Imagine that you're going to hike Mt Everest, would you just take to the mountain without setting up your base camp or preparation? No! That would be suicide. You can only reach the top with solid preparation, planning and support.

When Edmund Hilary made it up to the summit of Mt Everest, he wasn't alone. Tenzin Norgay, a local Sherpa acted as a guide and friend along the trek. If not for Tenzin's experience and local knowledge, who knows if Hilary would be in the history books of today. Without a base camp you don't have the planning and support required. That's why my formula begins with the foundation first, for without it, you can't build anything lasting.

The first step is the most important because it builds a strong foundation from which to build on. Then you keep building up from solid ground rather than sinking sand. Taking the first step is so important and needs to be acknowledged and applauded. In order to receive help, you need to *first* know that you need help and are willing to reach out and *ask* for help! This should not be overlooked.

For success to occur you need to get yourself into the right state of mind. If you're not in the right state of mind, you can easily detour, get distracted or waste a lot of time. You can actually feel more challenged, overwhelmed and frustrated because you let your mind run all over you rather than you being in control of it.

THE ABC'S OF SETTING OF THE MIND

Setting of the Mind is made up of three parts or stages: **A, B** and **C**. All stages are required to establish a good foundation with a strong and positive mindset.

> *"Your state of mind is everything."*
> — Bruce Lee —

STAGE A = AWARENESS. ACCEPTANCE. ACKNOWLEDGE. ASK.

Like I said in the beginning of this chapter, if you want to step on any fear, you need to be aware of the fear you are facing and be willing to want to know how to step on it. Only when you are **Aware** of the existence of the fear, can you then identify it as a problem or challenge that needs to be solved.

And only when you **Acknowledge** the need and want to solve it, will you be compelled to **Ask** for help.

See the cycle? If you don't take the first step by becoming **Aware**, you can't get off first base. The first tiny step builds momentum to attempt the next step.

Like my example with Sam earlier, when you keep delaying or postponing a problem, that sensitivity, that discomfort, that pain can actually lead to a disaster. Just ask any qualified dentist or look into any medical literature and you'll find this reoccurring theme — if you leave a problem untreated, it will get worse. In fact, it can be fatal.

For example, an infection can become cellulitis. This infection can actually invade the vital organs. So when a person like Sam decides to let the simple toothache develop into something more serious, over time, the person can be severely compromised or even die from the disease. So you can't ignore a problem. It's best to treat the root cause, not the symptoms.

Other problems can be like this too. You might think that some issues are too small to cause a problem, but many full-blown problems begin this way. Think of a smoker having one or two cigarettes per day. Does that stay at one or two? No! Why? Besides nicotine being an addictive substance, it's also because small actions go on to become bigger behaviours that become habits. Or perhaps it's eating greasy food every day. For the first week it's okay but years of the same fatty diet ends in disease.

Fear has the same type of pattern. What can begin as a small fear can in fact become a life-debilitating phobia.

It is very important to be **Aware** of the existence of a problem and be willing to deal with it. It's a nice feeling to just kick it and be done with it. **Awareness** allows you to **Acknowledge** that you would like it to be resolved, that you no longer want it to control or influence you.

This leads you to be able to **Accept** and **Ask** for help. And once you **Ask** for help you get **Answers**!

STAGE B = BELONGING. BELIEF. BONDING.

When you go through Stage A, you begin to see something very important. You begin to see that there are people who are more than happy to help you and that you are not alone.

One of the most popular songs ever written was called 'You'll Never Walk Alone'. It's become an anthem for soccer teams and other sporting clubs. In fact, since its debut in the movie *Carousel* by Rodgers and Hammerstein way back in 1945, some of the most famous singers in the world have covered it such as Frank Sinatra, Roy Orbison, Elvis Presley, Johnny Cash and the list goes on.

But why is it so popular? I believe because it speaks right into the heart of everyone. It bonds us to each other and makes us feel united rather than alone. As I said earlier, we are born to bond and born to belong. We want to know that we aren't alone.

Knowing that you are not alone is critical because it allows you to reach out and embrace a deeper sense of **Belonging**; it helps you feel safe and supported by people who truly value and care about you. Feeling that you belong is important in shaping your relationship with others by establishing good **Bonding** with positive and caring people around you.

If you want to step on your fear, you need to **Believe** that you can. **Believe** that you are not the only one experiencing this fear or problem right now. Many people have or are going through something similar, or will sooner or later.

*"Just cos you can't see the air,
doesn't stop you from breathing.
Just cos you can't see God,
doesn't stop you from believing.*

*Not for the past but
for the future.
Not for the failures but
for the dreams.
Not for the imperfections but
for the possibilities.*

*Hallelujah.
Praise the Lord. Amen."*

— Dr Catherine Yang —

Believing is a powerful force. **Bonding** is equally powerful.

When you find that **Bond** with a person or a group, it feels amazing. It feels as though somebody is actually talking in your language; like they're on the same page, the same wavelength as you. It's an incredibly uplifting invisible power: a force of connection.

The word *bonding* is so powerful in dentistry too. We use the word to also mean a bonding agent. When we do a filling, we get rid of the decay or nasties, clean the cavity and prepare the site before we put that beautiful nice white filling into the hole. We apply a bonding agent. What does that do? It is that chemical reaction that creates a strong vice-like bonding to hold new things in place. Where there was once a void, it becomes whole again. The metaphor with real-life bonding is the same. A bonding forms a 'sticking together' through thick and thin.

Building a **Bridge of Trust** with yourself and others is imperative to help you gain confidence and embark on your life's journey. (I discuss more about building the **Bridge of Trust** in the following **Tools** section).

POSITIVE PEOPLE VERSUS TOXIC PEOPLE

Bonding and **Belonging** doesn't mean that you just glue yourself to any new person or group. It's important to have positive bonds and a positive sense of belonging. It is equally and critically important to dissociate yourself from toxic and negative people who cannot add any value to you but rather they keep throwing curveballs at you.

Positive people will help you to find at least one solution for every problem but negative people always have at least one problem for every solution.

You don't have to associate yourself with people who actually make you feel down, put you down or just bring you down. Don't hang around with people who fill up your day or life with toxic ideas or negativity. Your life is too precious. You know, no matter what goes on in the world, the most precious and irreplaceable currency is time.

Find people who can trust and treasure and value you, not people who devalue you or make you feel drained and depressed. You don't have time for that. It's very important that you find a sense of **Belonging**, or a **Bond** you can feel safe with. It's a beautiful thing and we are wired to bond.

A 2015 study by Harvard Business School showed something many of us intuitively feel. Researchers Michael Housman and Dylan Minor, studied 'toxic workers' and their impact in the workforce.[8]

Their research from over 50,000 employees shows that toxic workers are the reason why so many employees leave an organisation. They in fact do a lot of harm with their attitudes and behaviours. They generate a negative environment and increase a company's training costs, due to the fact that many employees resign because of them.

According to Dr. Housman, toxic behaviour also becomes somewhat contagious and others begin acting equally toxic. This creates a negative culture in the organisation and has far-reaching consequences for the business and other people's health.

In many instances, the boss or company owner doesn't even know the impact that a small toxic culture begins to create. Sometimes it goes unnoticed because the boss may be looking at income figures or other parameters for how the business is doing. You can have productive people who are also toxic. It's important to pay close attention to toxic cultures, attitudes and people so you can rid yourself of them.

On the flipside, leading expert Kim Cameron, the William Russell Kelly Professor of Management and Organizations at the Ross School of Business at the University of Michigan knows the power of positive people and practices.[9] His research and books all point to the

---

8   Housman, Michael, and Dylan Minor. "Toxic Workers." Harvard Business School Working Paper, No. 16-057, October 2015. http://nrs.harvard.edu/urn-3:HUL.InstRepos:23481825

9   Cameron, K., Mora, G., Leutscher, T., & Calarco, M. (2011). Effects of Positive Practices on Organizational Effectiveness. *The Journal of Applied Behavioral Science*, 47(3), 266–308. https://doi.org/10.1177/0021886310395514

importance of a positive and virtuous culture in the workplace (and other environments). He talks to businesses all over the globe about the requirement to implement positive leadership practices that directly enhance and increase profitability, happiness, productivity and employee retention and morale.

Similar positive psychological intervention studies have also found that individuals' practice of kindness and expressing gratitude to others enhanced their subjective and social wellbeing.[10]

Yes! Gratitude and kindness does positively impact people and it's a natural remedy we can all use.

So **Bond** with those that also support and enhance your wellbeing. Build something with like-minded loving individuals and avoid toxic bonding, they will only bring you down and keep you down.

---

10 Seligman, M. E. P., Steen, T. A., Park, N., & Peterson, C. (2005). Positive Psychology Progress: Empirical Validation of Interventions. *American Psychologist*, 60(5), 410–421. https://doi.org/10.1037/0003-066X.60.5.410

> Surround yourself with only people who are going to lift you higher.
>
> **OPRAH WINFREY**

STAGE C = COMPLIMENT. CONFIDENCE. COURAGE.

If you want to lead a fulfilling life, you need to learn how to give yourself **Compliments** for taking the journey to **S.T.E.P. on Fear**. It takes some hard work and strong faith to make progress through the stages. As the motivational speaker Simon Sinek said, "Working hard for something we do not care about is called stress, working hard for something we love is called passion."

Give yourself permission to be complimented. **Compliment** yourself for taking the first step. Compliment yourself for your bravery and courage. That first step is always the hardest. Research shows that receiving compliments improves our ability to perform tasks and acts as reward stimuli for our brains similar to receiving a cash prize.[11] Our brains love compliments (even from ourselves) and we all need a little encouragement along the way.

> Use sentiments like:
> *Well done*
> *Good job*
> *I'm proud of you*
> *You're doing a wonderful job*
> *You are kicking goals*
> *Excellent effort*
> *Keep going*

Once you take that first step and gain more **Confidence** to put fear under your feet and step on it, you start to notice many great opportunities and tools and resources around you that

---

[11] Sugawara SK, Tanaka S, Okazaki S, Watanabe K, Sadato N (2012) Social Rewards Enhance Offline Improvements in Motor Skill. *PLoS ONE* 7(11): e48174. https://doi.org/10.1371/journal.pone.0048174

you didn't see before. When you are trapped and let fear get the better of you, you get tunnel vision; you can't see clearly, you can't even see the opportunities or people around you that can actually help you.

When you give yourself a compliment and a pat on the back to say, "Great job," you set yourself up to increase your self-confidence. You become more **Confident** in your ability to take action. Now of course, you also need a dose of **Courage** sometimes along the journey.

Courage isn't the absence of fear but is to continue moving forward despite the fear. **Courage** is in the effort to try and pursue goals and dreams, to be brave and courageous. In his famous 'Citizenship in a Republic' speech Theodore Roosevelt talked about courage. He said:

> *It is not the critic who counts: not the man who points out how the strong man stumbles or where the doer of deeds could have done better. The credit belongs to the man who is actually in the arena, whose face is marred by dust and sweat and blood, who strives valiantly, who errs and comes up short again and again, because there is no effort without error or shortcomings, but who knows the great enthusiasms, the great devotions, who spends himself for a worthy cause; who, at the best, knows, in the end, the triumph of high achievement, and who, at the worst, if he fails, at least he fails while daring greatly, so that his place shall never be with those cold and timid souls who knew neither victory or defeat.* [12]

---

[12] Theodore Roosevelt 'Citizenship in a Republic' (Speech at the Sorbonne, Paris, April 23, 1910)

Setting your Mind to instil **Courage** is setting your mind to try, to give effort, to apply yourself wholeheartedly without the promise of reward or success. But of course, those that try are already halfway to achieving this.

By making your choice to **Compliment** yourself, to gain **Confidence** and be **Courageous** is a small win every time and is worthy of celebration. Remember that a giant leap for mankind started with one man's small step. Let's turn fear into cheers!

Celebrate yourself every time you make a small victory. Celebrate every time you use **Confidence, Courage** and **Compliments**. Stay in the game. Treasure your life because you're worth it. Don't waste your magnificence.

STEP 2
TOOLS

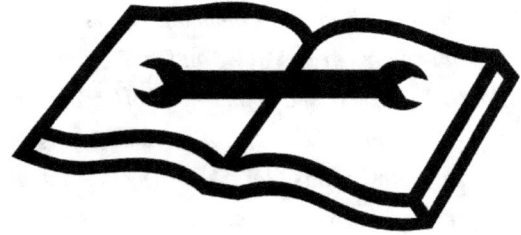

Once you step on solid ground with a strong and positive mindset, your perspective starts to evolve as you see things from higher ground, at a level different from your old self (away from those limiting beliefs, doubts and your comfort zone). Instead of worrying and feeling lost, you begin to feel excitement. You also begin to notice the new tools, resources and opportunities around you. It opens your vision to what is available for you.

As the adage goes, 'You don't know what you don't know', therefore you won't find what you need or want if you don't know what you are looking for. This leaves many people deciding to settle for less because they are too afraid to step outside their comfort zone and explore and discover what they truly deserve. Remember, the comfortable zone is cleverly masked as a 'compromised zone' that limits your imagination, sabotages your dreams, doubts your faith, restrains your growth and wastes your life.

So why don't we see these new opportunities and tools until we set our mind right?

It's because when we get stressed or feel restricted, we get tunnel vision. Tunnel vision gives us a restricted view. Physiologically, when the body produces high levels of adrenaline under extreme panic, stress or anger it can cause temporary tunnel vision. Alcohol and drugs have also been shown to have an effect on peripheral (the outer edges of the visual field) loss of vision. The physical visual impairment can create obstacles in life, affect the orientation of the body and the mind and cause more fear psychologically, mentally and spiritually.

Some high-ranking trainers of police officers and paramedics train their squads in how to reduce tunnel vision. They know that when threatened, the body's fight-or-flight response is triggered and this can lead to a narrow focus. A narrow focus prevents them from seeing other threats or opportunities outside of the small focus point. This is part of the reason why they are trained to approach all scenes in a calm way and breathe deeply — to reduce the amount of stress hormone and narrow-lens perspective.

I want you to try this exercise: cover the upper, outer edges of your eyes by bringing your hands to the sides of your forehead just above the temple areas. Notice how much of your vision is reduced, and what options are being blocked from you. Even in your most familiar place at home or work, vision impairment can lead to loss of direction, lack of confidence and feelings of doubts or worries spiralling downwards (and in some extreme cases, people can feel trapped in the dark abyss).

> Check out the Interactive book to see Cath demonstrate this in a video at deanpublishing.com/steponfear

THE ABUNDANCE OF TOOLS

Tools, resources and opportunities are there for those who are prepared and ready to utilise them. After you have set your mind and built a vision for the future, you will see an abundance of tools available.

There are two words in English that I find fascinating: one is *useful*, the other is *helpful*. When I was learning English these definitions would always puzzle me. What was the difference between being useful and being helpful, I wondered.

After a few years of pondering this, I began to understand. Think of a product or a service that is useful and often only solves a one-time need or request. This is why you usually associate single-use disposable items as useful rather than helpful. It's wonderful to use an environmentally friendly reusable bag but sometimes you want to buy more than the bag can actually carry and so one bag is useful but not completely helpful. Usefulness does have a value, but doesn't create a lasting big impact.

Helpful however opens up a totally different world. Helpful items or products mean that you can go back and use them over again. This happens in businesses too. For example, the difference between a local dentist who is useful just because they happened to be open on the day of your emergency when you needed a quick-fix versus the helpful dentist whom you have trusted with your ongoing care and who came recommended to you by others.

Tools can be useful or helpful, but for long-term gains it's best to look at the bigger view and see if your tools will serve the long game or your short sprint.

Being useful = usually a short term, quick fix and choice of convenience for single-use. Usually disposable and indistinguishable, normally no loyalty is built or earned.

Being helpful = usually long-term, added value, and choice of trust from good experience or word of mouth. Usually irreplaceable, unique and special and often is sought for advice and is highly valued and appreciated. Normally loyalty is built and earned.

When dealing with fear, a useful tool may be helpful temporarily but it may not be the best strategy for the long haul. For example, I once knew a lady who suffered from anxiety. She was afraid of her business failing and couldn't sleep at night. She went to her doctor and discussed her issues. He prescribed sleeping pills to help ease her anxiety and give her a good night's sleep.

For the first two weeks she felt better. But the core problem (her failing business) was not addressed and so the short-term 'useful' fix did nothing in the long run. If anything, the problem became worse as she began to rely on her 'quick fix' pills that numbed out her underlying problem (her failing business).

Now, I'm not implying that this was good/bad or right/wrong. Everyone has different ways of coping with problems, but it does illustrate my point — what is useful has a short life span and what is helpful has a lifetime value. What would have been most helpful to her do you think?

Imagine if she found an amazing business mentor and succeeded in keeping her business. She would be less anxious, sleep well and have a thriving business for the rest of her life. Furthermore, the right mentor or teacher often has a lifetime of wisdom to offer and they could help her over and over again. This is the powerful difference between useful and helpful. Look for what will help you first.

THE RIGHT TOOLS

While patience is a virtue, when you invest time to set a strong and positive mindset as a good and solid foundation, the right tools are a bonus opportunity for accelerated growth. **Tools** to look for can be such things as:

- A book to read
- A course to attend
- A teacher or mentor (when the student is ready the teacher appears)
- A great team (teamwork makes dream work)
- Online help — digital, apps, equipment
- A new opportunity for growth

The three main components in **Tools** are: **Timing**, **Trust** and **Training**.

Use good **Timing** to recognise the helpful **Tools**, which you can **Trust** and use to **Train** yourself in order to progress and keep stepping up and advancing forward for a better and healthier life.

TIMING IS EVERYTHING

We learn many things in life but we cannot learn everything at the same time. Learning in life comes from making decisions. A timely decision can alter the smallest moment in life by recognising the potential resources and opportunities to reach your goals when they come towards you. Goals that, at other times seemed unreachable.

For example, I always had a big vision to run a successful business for good but I thought I was too small to make it. I had dreamed of becoming a dentist since I was 12 years old. I believe that everyone smiles in the same language and I wanted to restore thousands of beautiful and healthy smiles to the world.

> *"Everyone smiles in the same language."*
> **— George Carlin —**

When we founded Chats Dental in 2013, we only had one dentist (me), one dental assistant (an all-rounder answering phone calls, booking appointments, clinical assistance and general duties) and one practice manager (my husband, doing the bookkeeping and paying bills). Being a small clinic located in a highly competitive metropolitan suburb of Sydney, we worked six days a week with extended hours and hardly had any time to rest. In spite of our endless hard work, we could hardly make ends meet and were on the verge of burning out.

When opportunities came to us for hiring additional staff, I thought that we couldn't afford to pay more staff. When opportunities came to us to implement a comprehensive dental treatment plan, I thought that we couldn't afford to invest in high-tech equipment for delivering the result more efficiently.

My fear held me back from making the critical decision *timely*, so a lot of good opportunities came and went and so my big dream drifted further away. I was so afraid to lose my business, my job, and my dream.

In July 2017, in my desperation I attended a huge non-dental business event, wishing to turn around my struggling business (by the way, if you think medical terminology is hard for non-medical personnel to understand, I can tell you that the business jargon was impossible for me to comprehend!).

That was when I first met Mr Paul Dunn, the co-founder of B1G1, a social enterprise and global giving initiative.

Mr Dunn is a great speaker with a great heart making a significant difference to the world. Together with Masami Sato, the founder of B1G1, their ingenious idea of creating smile-impacts around the world by embedding giving-activities into everyday business operations, is helping everyday people and everyday businesses of every size in countries across the globe.

I was amazed by Mr Dunn's main presentation however while he was on stage, he made a joke about one of his crowned teeth having come loose during dinner the night before and that it could slip out of his mouth at any time during his speech. He asked the audience sitting closer to the stage to watch out for it and kindly return the tooth to him for a fix with his dentist once he returned home to Singapore shortly.

Based on my 20 years of clinical experience, I could sense that this unexpected dental issue was really concerning Mr Dunn. At the registration for the event earlier, I knew I was the only dentist attending this non-dental business conference with some hundreds of business entrepreneurs there that night. I knew by the time Mr Dunn finished his speech presentation, it would be impossible for him to find an experienced dentist still working late on a Saturday night in Sydney.

At that moment, I knew I had a decision to make in life. I knew I had to step on my own fear:
- The fear of being unknown (a nobody)
- The fear of being small
- The fear of rejection.

I knew it was time for me to:
- Help a person in need with my expertise
- Serve a person who has served so many others
- Open my clinic after hours and create an impact.

I called our one and only dental assistant, Ting — who also has the most beautiful heart to help and serve people — to open up our small clinic, ready to welcome our distinguished guest. I plucked up my courage and walked over to Mr Dunn after his speech presentation. I introduced myself and asked him if I could have the privilege to serve him by helping with his dental issue. Mr Dunn was stunned at first but graciously accepted my offer.

Timing is everything. Ting and I had one of the best times at work on that night. Not only did we do a great job professionally with wonderful outcomes but we learned so much about doing "business for good" from Mr Dunn's visit to our small clinic. To date, Chats Dental is successfully operational with four dentists and eight team members, serving the community and creating smile impacts in the world.

TRUST

Trust is a verb meaning 'to believe'. **Trust** is active through believing.

In STEP 1 **Setting of the Mind**, I explained **Bonding** with others will give you a sense of **Belonging**. **Bonding** is established by building the **Bridge of Trust** with the people who believe in you and help you to believe in yourself. This Bridge of Trust not only gives you the **Confidence** and **Courage** to step on your fear, but also increases your connection with people and places and your feeling of belonging.

Within STEP 2 **Tools**, **Trust** is built on telling the truth, and trust is strongly connected to love. In love, there is no fear.

> *"There is no fear in love."*
> — 1 John 4:18, The Bible (NIV) —

Let me give you a practical example from my own experience. My six-year-old son Ethan loved playing with Lego. Sometimes he would spend hours building something using his imagination and creativity. The extended time he spent focusing on the tiny building blocks in his room worried his grandparents in regard to the indoor lighting and the effects on his eyes. My husband and I were more concerned about his lack of sleep and often had to remind him to pack up for bed.

One night I caught him again staying up with the dim lighting in his room, building his new invention in spite of his promise to go to bed. I was angry with him for not keeping his word so I told him that he broke my trust in him. With tears trickling down his tiny face, he said, "Mummy, I am really sorry and I love you very much. What can I do to make you feel better?"

I told him, "I will always love you because you are my son. But being my son, you still need to build the **Bridge of Trust** with me."

I further explained that building a good and sturdy bridge requires great effort, and it is only strong and stable when the two sides are brought together to meet in the middle. This requires the right choice of care, materials and tools. He understood the metaphor for building a bridge as his Lego creations were quite exceptional and he knew a poorly built bridge could easily fall.

To build a **Bridge of Trust** requires care, precision and accuracy; it requires training, timing, focus, and faith. Simply by loving the idea of building a bridge is not enough. Without commitment and perseverance, the **Bridge of Trust** cannot be built or will not last.

It's like playing with Lego blocks: simply by loving Lego and the imaginative play it ignites is great, but without the trust (action with the belief that you can achieve your idea), creativity will not turn into an innovation.

After our chat, Ethan rubbed his tired eyes, nodded and crawled into his bed. That was the beginning of the **Bridge of Trust** project between my son and me.

> When I am afraid,
> I will trust in you.
> In God, whose
> word I praise,
> in God I trust;
> I will not be afraid.
>
> **PSALM 56:3–4,
> THE BIBLE (NIV)**

TRAINING

Through **Training** you can master the hard skills and soft skills that are required before you progress further onto the next step.

Training requires learning, dedication and perseverance. Hard skills can be taught and soft skills can be nurtured. Both can be trained and maintained provided that the training is comprehensive, systemic, practical and meaningful.

An eagerness to learn and willingness for growth is essential to master both the hard and soft skills from the utilisation of the **Tools** to **S.T.E.P. on Fear**.

A burning desire to learn is the starting point for successful training and gets the result for any skillset. A weak desire to learn cannot produce sustainable good results. A burning desire intensifies your intention to master a skillset and it motivates you to commit to the training process.

For example, a little baby learns to walk from watching other people walk and developing a burning desire to learn to walk too. The baby is programmed to explore new concepts and is eager to learn new skills. Longing and enthusiasm for growth brings your commitment to a higher level, that is, dedication. Dedication is about your passion for performing what you commit to do and agree with.

A candle burns when a chemical reaction produces heat and light energy. The physical properties of candles cause them to burn differently, but they all require oxygen to keep on burning. Desire to learn and to grow, is *our* oxygen and keeps our flame burning.

Training is important because it helps build confidence. Think of a professional pianist or a fantastic carpenter, without tools and training, they would not be the professionals they have become.

For example, our team at Chats Dental are given tools and training. They aren't expected to know everything themselves. We use systems, templates and scripts to help them. I use them myself too. We have a script and templates for many things like questions, enquiries, and conflicts or cancelled appointments. We even have a template and script for a greeting.

This is not to make our team into robots of course; it's to give them tools and training that support them. They don't have to worry about what they should or shouldn't say because it's provided for them as a guide.

We even practise our soft skills like listening and care. We don't expect these to be inbuilt in everyone, but they can be trained and taught.

Each one of us is unique and special in our own way. It is up to us to have a desire to learn, to kindle our passion, and to persist with training for achieving good and sustainable results.

Perseverance is to do all it takes with a steadfast belief and continuous effort without giving up despite difficulty or delay in achieving success.

> Strength and growth come only through continued effort and struggle.
>
> **NAPOLEON HILL**

STEP 3
ENJOYMENT

As you continue to **S.T.E.P. on Fear**, you feel less fearful (fear-*less*) and feel better about yourself. You start to enjoy life because you can see good results and great outcomes by overcoming your fear and turning fear into cheers!

It is not just a sense of relief from feeling overwhelmed and burnt-out, but also a sense of happiness for bringing out the best version of you and visualizing your dreams into reality. Instead of chasing after happiness, it is best to receive happiness as a gift with the **Enjoyment** you experience.

In STEP 3 **Enjoyment**, there are three key points to enjoy true happiness: **Emphasis**, **Experience**, and **Empowerment**.

Emphasis on what truly matters is the first key point to enjoy true happiness. True happiness is about having people around you to be happy with you, not just by you or for you. When I was a child, I used to think my happiest moment was when I felt my parents were happy. With a farming background, my dad grew up in generational poverty and was the first university graduate in his family and the only school graduate among his siblings.

At the age of nineteen, my dad and mum left their small town, from the southernmost Pingtung county to the big capital city, Taipei in the northern part of Taiwan. Travelling over 380km along the west coast, my parents wanted to start a new chapter in life and be able to provide for their new family with better education, more opportunities and a better lifestyle. I grew up with many things and I never had to help out with any housework. My parents only wanted my brother and me to focus on our studies. To them, education is the key to breaking the cycle of poverty.

Even though the economy was tough back then, my parents never let my brother and me feel poor. We were fed well and clothed warmly. We never stayed in one apartment for more than five years and we moved places every few years. Dad and Mum worked very hard so that we could eventually own our apartment in the big capital city, Taipei.

Dad always likes to share with us his childhood stories and remind us of how important it is to keep chasing your dream and never give up. I liked to see his smile when he was feeling proud of his achievements and I carried it on, thinking I could be happy when he was proud of my achievements too.

When I received my university awards on stage, I always felt great seeing my parents' smiling faces in the audience. When I didn't score well in my exams at school, I felt terrible with guilt and thoughts of disappointing my parents although they never gave me any pressure on my studies. I focused on other people's happy faces, rather than an emphasis on what truly matters.

Fast forward to 1991 when my parents sold everything they owned to move to Australia. We were so excited to build our new Australian dream. As I mentioned previously, it was not easy at all. The language barrier and cultural differences affected almost every aspect of our new life. The challenges were enormous but they remained focused on what mattered most — our future and happiness.

EMPHASIS

Emphasis on what truly matters. So, what does truly matter?

You! I am not talking about being selfish and ignoring people around you. On the contrary, I am talking about being responsive to your true happiness so that people around you are happy with you. Don't just blame other people for your misery. Don't just complain about your burden. Do something about it. Take action and **S.T.E.P. on Fear**!

In my view, 'blame' does not serve well and is a waste of time. I spell the word 'blame' as 'bla-me' meaning an incomprehensible gibberish (as in 'blah, blah, blah') that only matters to 'me'. It is important to know where your **Emphasis** is in life. You are worthy. You matter. Your true happiness is where your **Emphasis** needs to be.

Ask yourself where you are on your **Emphasis** scale? Do you prioritise yourself and your self-care? Do you matter?

A mother of three young children is a familiar visitor to our dental clinic. She came frequently to accompany her children for their various dental needs but whenever our receptionist asked if she would like to make a dental check-up appointment for herself, she always declined politely with a reason that she was too busy looking after the family.

One day when she came in as an emergency new patient with a severe toothache, we found out that she had been putting it off for months until she couldn't bear the pain. Although it was fortunate that she was treated timely to avoid facial cellulitis, it would have been so much better with routine dental check-ups and preventive measures. I told her,

"You matter the most to your young family, and your health and well-being bring true happiness to enjoy together with your loved ones."

At work, I often see many mothers doing the same. They bring their kids in for their routine dental check-ups, or dental treatments but hardly remember their own dental check-ups. Even in the situation of dental emergencies, mothers still have to try very hard to work through their budgets and busy schedules in order to fit in their urgent dental care.

In those moments, I saw there was often a discrepancy between a mother's self-value and priorities in life. I will often stop talking about dental problems and start asking mums what's important in their life; kids, family, career, dreams? Once I discover what is important to her in life, I ask her to consider the important role she plays in everyone's lives: raising children, building relationships, planning for the next stage in life, and to understand her amazing self-worth and the value of looking after herself.

A great mum always puts her own needs last by serving the others first. A great mum needs to be healthy and happy too though. Many families depend on the mum to look after every big and small thing in life. Without the mum, suddenly the family doesn't know how to function or what to do if the mum is sick and feeling unwell. A great mum deserves to be well looked after so that she can continue to enjoy looking after those important to her in life. It's like the safety spiel from the flight attendant, "Put your own oxygen mask on first so you can help others."

EXPERIENCE

> *"Every new experience brings its own maturity and a greater clarity of vision."*
> **— Indira Gandhi —**

Experience growth. The key element in growing is to enjoy the experience in life by embracing your emotions so that you can **S.T.E.P. on Fear** and turn fear into cheers! Fear is part of life and you do not need to feel bad about it. The fear of learning new things may be daunting at first but if you **Emphasise** the great outcomes you can enjoy when you accomplish the learning course, you will start to **Experience** the happiness of growth along the way.

This is like learning to grow plants from seeds or to breed chickens — after you sow the seed or while you wait for an egg to hatch — you won't know for sure how it will turn out and you could have some degree of fear for the unknown, the unexpected and the uncontrolled. But when you witness the seed sprouting or the egg hatching, you will be so excited to experience the growth. It may not be comfortable to break through the soil or the eggshell but it's all worth it because of the amount of joy that comes after.

As the great author Brian Tracy said, "Every experience in your life is being orchestrated to teach you something you need to know to move forward."

Great experiences breed great outcomes. **Enjoying** yourself along the road is crucial.

A great source of knowledge is experience. You can't experience things through the intellect only; you need the physical experience of doing things. For example, you can intellectually learn all about swimming but until your body learns how to actually swim it's only an intellectual understanding. You could in fact drown without experience.

Experience embodies knowledge in a way that the intellect can't. You can learn about the elements in water and how hydrogen and oxygen behave, but that can't quench your thirst — only the experience of drinking water can satisfy you.

> "The only source of knowledge is experience."
> **— Albert Einstein —**

EMPOWERMENT

With personal value and self-worth, **Empowerment** gives lasting enjoyment with long-term happiness. The Cambridge dictionary describes empowerment as, 'The process of gaining freedom and power to do what you want or to control what happens to you.'[13]

Empowerment has also been described by leading psychologists as, "A form of power that helps people gain control over their own lives."[14] And as, "A social process that fosters power in people, their communities, and in their society."[15]

Sometimes our power diminishes when we seek the need for approval. This approval seeking behaviour is often instilled in people from early childhood onwards, seeking the approval of parents, teachers, elders, spouses, bosses and friends. However we must begin to determine our own

---

13 Cambridge dictionary online. 2020. Available at <https://dictionary.cambridge.org/dictionary/english/empowerment> (Accessed 17 September 2020).

14 Hur M.H. (2013) Empowerment. In: Gellman M.D., Turner J.R. (eds) *Encyclopedia of Behavioral Medicine*. Springer, New York, NY

15 Page, N., & Czuba, C. E. (1999). Empowerment: What is it? *Journal of Extension*, 37(5), 24–32.

self-worth and direction in order to feel most empowered. As Alice Walker, author of the Pulitzer prize winning book *The Colour Purple* said, "The most common way people give up their power is by thinking they don't have any."

When you find your self-identity, define your personal value, determine your self-worth, and be true to yourself, you feel empowered to embark on a journey of creating your own fulfilling life. And when you can extend that approach and **Empower** people around you by giving, delegating and trusting, people will join with you and participate in your vision with unity and joy.

Learn how to Empower yourself so you can experience your own greatness.

Go to the Interactive book at **deanpublishing.com/steponfear** and watch Dr Catherine Yang's video.

STEP 4
PURPOSE

"Did you know that every human being is created with a purpose and that they have a responsibility to not only discover their purpose but also to fulfil it?"

— Zig Ziglar —

As you **S.T.E.P. on Fear** through the processes from **Setting of the Mind**, to utilising the helpful **Tools**, and experiencing the growth and great outcomes with **Enjoyment**, the **Purpose** of the journey is revealed.

A life driven by purpose, passion and drive is a life well spent. People need to have a purpose in life to go on living. Some may start with a small goal and some may have a big vision. Regardless of the size and the kind of purpose, it needs to be something the person will enjoy working towards.

Your birth was no mistake and your existence is not an accident. Every one of us was created for a purpose. You deserve to appreciate and enjoy the abundance in life. Without any purpose, life withers away. Having a purpose helps you to grow and learn throughout your life.

A purpose-driven life gives you:
- Compassion for others
- Courage to practise self-awareness and **S.T.E.P. on Fear**
- An ability to identify your fears/problems/challenges in life
- An acute awareness to recognise the tools and resources you need
- Gratitude for the life you have
- A willingness to propagate your wisdom to others.

Before I knew how to **S.T.E.P. on Fear**, I felt miserable when I was in a dark place mentally. I doubted the meaning of my existence and I questioned the purpose of my life. It wasn't pleasant and I was in despair. I didn't have much self-worth and I felt embarrassed by my net-worth.

I want to share with you some examples of my dark times and places so you can relate and know you are not alone in overcoming your worries. Often these times involved feeling alone and that there was no way out (until I found a **Purpose**). Some of my dark times have been:
- Trying to settle into a new lifestyle, unable to pick up the new language and knowing that my parents were struggling too.
- Knowing that I needed help but not knowing how to ask.
- Not wanting to add more burden to my parents who also needed help but they didn't know who to ask and they sometimes felt embarrassed to reach out.
- Having conflicts living with the in-laws in one household, (we lived with my father-in-law ever since we got married, and my mum-in-law flew back and forth between Sydney and Taipei on her terms) and I found it very

difficult to explain and talk with my husband about my true inner feelings.

We lived with my father-in-law for 11 years until he passed away and every time when my mum-in-law came to Sydney, I had to go through a lot of inner-self-talk and adjustments. In the darkest moment, I questioned myself; *why did I get myself into this? I would be fine just being single on my own*, I thought to myself. But then I was scared by my other fear of living with my parents for the rest of my life if I didn't get married or managed to move out independently. Dark times have also included:
- Parenthood: it's not easy and actual parenting is hard, especially living in an environment with so many different opinions, distractions and family influences and backgrounds.
- Running a business: has had many challenges and difficulties.

Chats Dental was founded during Australia's mini-recession time in 2013. Even the lenders and dental sales suppliers of IT and software systems and expensive dental equipment wondered why we chose to start-up at that time and warned us about the burst of an economic bubble.

I was pregnant with my second child in 2013 and I literally worked until the day before my son was born. During his first few months, I was dashing in and out of the workplace to breastfeed him, and managing work, staff, family (husband and my 2.5-year-old daughter), in-laws (both were living with us), and my own parents (living in the neighbourhood). I felt that I was burning out but I had also burned any escape plan and there was no turning back.

In my own examples of living in a dark place, I needed a **Purpose** to make a decision to **S.T.E.P. on Fear** whenever I felt a fear (a change, a threat, a disturbance in life, or a fear of the uncertainties for the future). The purpose does not need to be big or far ahead or for the long-term. The purpose can be small, near, and for the short-term. The most important thing is the purpose needs to have an outcome that the person enjoys when the goal is reached.

> Dreaming to do great things is not fulfilling until the dream becomes a reality.
>
> **DR CATHERINE YANG**

FINDING PURPOSE

Finding a purpose in life is not an easy task, but it is essential for living a life with meaning. A person always needs a purpose to keep on living; otherwise life becomes boring and devoid of meaning.

Anxiety, depression, along with suicidal thoughts can be prevented, eradicated and treated by restoring self-worth and life purpose. In order to live a life and visualise a brighter future on the way, a person needs to believe that he or she is worthy and deserves it. Self-value increases instantly when the person feels needed, wanted and loved. A person starts to value their self-worth when they see their higher purpose in life.

Creating a **purpose statement** is one way to clarify your direction and to feel empowered. My personal purpose statement to date would be: *To help people restore their sustainable healthy smiles so that they can enjoy life wholeheartedly.*

When your heart can shine through your smile, you have stepped on your fear and turned fear into cheers!

CREATING YOUR OWN PERSONAL PURPOSE STATEMENT

So how do you know what your purpose is?

You can define 'a purpose' for life or you can also create a purpose for moments or events *in* life. Our purpose often changes as we experience more of life. When I became a mum I had several purposes: to be a great mum, to run a great business and to be a wonderful partner to my husband. I became multi-purposeful.

Some young people still need to explore their life to find their true vocational calling but you can still have purpose-filled moments, goals and dreams — no matter how big or small. Let me give you a personal example.

My little girl, Sarah, was given a school assignment to give a speech in front of the class. The speech was about what you would say or do if you were the Prime Minister of Australia and it followed with a mini-school election. She had never given a speech before and this was all designed around scoring votes and being a compelling orator.

Now, Sarah is a naturally positive and happy girl who loves school, however this particular project had her rattled. She's not the type to put herself 'out there' or put her hand up. It was a real challenge for her to step outside her comfort zone and there was a real fear factor in doing it. She came home from school that day and said to my husband and me fearfully, "What am I going to do?"

I told Sarah, "You don't need to be scared, because this suits your beautiful character. You are always so willing to help people. If you have an intention to really help people then you can offer them your highest intention and make a positive impact in people's lives. This is a great purpose to have as you help more people."

I asked her to focus on making the world better and not to worry about anything else for now. I explained that being a leader isn't about bragging or boosting your ego, but a true leader is a great helper, to have a purpose beyond winning or popularity.

Sarah started to think and said, "Okay Mummy. But it's such a big job!"

I said, "Well, isn't it wonderful that you only need to present to your class of 25 people instead of 27 million people. This is a great starting point for you to practise."

We talked about using her speech as practice for the future and for making changes to improve people's lives. Practice for getting feedback from people and seeing if her speech touched people from all different backgrounds. I told her that the more feedback she gets, the stronger, wiser and better, she becomes.

So Sarah began to choose her mindset and soon enough she said, "Alright, I'm ready to try this. I need to accept this challenge."

She knew she was in a safe environment because her parents supported her and didn't expect her to be perfect. Sarah set her mindset to **Believe** in herself, and she knew she wasn't alone (**Bonding**). She soon was ready to take the second step, **Tools**.

So I asked her, "What do you need to help you do your speech?"

She thought about making the world better and researched her ideas. She asked us (my husband and me) for advice, and started to write some things down. She timed herself and practised saying her speech out loud.

I asked her, "What would make it helpful in the eyes of your audience? How will they be convinced by you?"

She started to think about her audience (fellow students) and wondered what they cared most about. She started to formulate some simple points, for example, having a variety of healthy food to choose from in the canteen. She also thought that people might not want to go to school every day (this was way before COVID so in many ways her proposition is actually coming true).

She said, "I would like to have the flexibility to give every student in class the ability to choose. They only need to come to school one day a week and the rest of the information can be online." She decided she needed something light and funny at the end, so lastly she wrote, "With Sarah Wong — you can't be wrong."

She then went to work and practised, practised, practised.

We really enjoyed watching her transform from a timid shy girl to **S.T.E.P. on her Fear** and overcome her initial tentativeness. When she finally delivered her speech in class, she was excited to share her ideas. She received the highest votes too. But it wasn't about the end result; it was who she became through the process. It was about finding her passion and her higher purpose to serve others.

Sarah couldn't have delivered a confident speech without first **Setting her Mind**. She would have remained uncertain and doubtful about what to say and whether she could face her classmates confidently. Without questioning them, those negative feelings would have grown bigger until her fear ruled her actions and mind.

Breaking down the process and her emotions into very separate steps, helped her understand what was really being asked of her. And also why it seemed overwhelming at first, after all she had never attempted anything like this.

After setting her mind, she used her own resources (experiences at school) as **Tools** and also asked advice from others (my husband and me), Sarah then built up a plan that **Emphasised** what was important to her (helping others and listening to their voices) and the speech project became an experience she really **Enjoyed** because it came from a place of **Purpose** so she could deliver it with passion.

Sarah's school project could have become an unpleasant experience that she wanted to forget but instead, by guiding her through how to **S.T.E.P. on Fear**, it became a wonderful learning experience that may have even sparked her on a course for her future, into a rewarding job serving people in the community with her passion, just as I was inspired at a young age to spread healthy smiles.

> Check out the Interactive book and learn how to Find Your Life Purpose with Dr Catherine Yang in a bonus video at **deanpublishing.com/steponfear**.

Don't delay in stepping on your fear. You have come this far in reading this book, which you should celebrate — *well done!* Now it's time to face the situations in your life that are holding you back and **S.T.E.P. on Fear.**

PART FOUR

S.T.E.P. ON Fear *Teams*

> When you are afraid, do the thing you are afraid of and soon you will lose your fear of it.
>
> **NORMAN VINCENT PEALE**

THE GIFT OF LEGACY

After embracing the **S.T.E.P on Fear** method for yourself, the possibilities become even more exciting. It is time to help others overcome fear and embrace their awesomeness in any setting.

I believe it is so important to pass on the good wisdom and knowledge you have gained in life so that you can not only help those people around you, in your personal life and your career, but also so you can extend out and help the wider community and the world.

Good people and good leaders love to help others. In fact, they strive to make others' lives better each and every day. This is their purpose, to give help. And they receive the blessing of happiness in return. They are purpose-filled people and don't see their job or position as a burden or duty, they see it as a blessing and a place of purpose from which to help.

I often remind people how lovely it is when someone comes to them for help. It doesn't matter what type of industry you work in or belong to. If you are in the healthcare business, trades, retail business or publishing business — whatever you do — you do the most important thing ever: you help people. You can feel glad that people are looking to you for help.

Your career, job or schooling should never be limited to the title of your position or job description because that mentality limits and prevents you from being your best. Think about people you know who are valued for that little 'extra' they bring to their role.

Think of it like this:
Would you like a highly skilled dentist to just do the job or would you prefer a highly skilled dentist who loves to help you feel safe and cared for in their chair?

Would you like a highly skilled teacher to just do the job or would you prefer a highly skilled teacher who loves to help you learn and see you grow?

Would you like a highly skilled counsellor to just do the job or would you prefer a highly skilled counsellor who cares about helping you to feel better for the long term?

You see, it's the unique 'essence' that you add to your job description and well-honed skills that makes you the best choice. It's the real love and care that you show, and pour into helping people that gives the experience extra flavour and sweetness.

It's that little unique sparkle and shine that you bring which makes your job or duty or role so important. People remember your care and will want to do the same for others.

The S.T.E.P on Fear *Teams* model can help leaders improve teams and workplaces in any situation. It follows the same 4-step process and can expand to all leaders within communities and even countries, helping teams to work more effectively and joyfully together.

TOGETHER EVERYONE ACHIEVES MORE

As well as the steps you are familiar with, this is an extended 'bonus' section specifically outlining extra hints and tips to help you within a group or team organisation.

You might be saying to yourself right now, "My team is working just fine, we don't need to change anything."

However remember everyone has fear in their life and it can subconsciously affect their confidence and therefore their actions and relationships in any situation. Applying the **S.T.E.P. on Fear** model is like a health check for your team or workplace. It is so helpful to address little problems before they turn into big ones.

It's also very important to be conscious of the words you choose when talking about the business. Within our team at our clinical practice, we deliberately use the word *our*, not *my* business — after all it is *our* business and we work towards *our* vision. If we don't all feel this way, we can't reach our goal.

DREAMS CAN BE FILLED WITH FEAR

Everyone within your team is somewhere along the path to their dreams. From the receptionist who might be saving money for a house in a different suburb to the manager who is working hard for a promotion, everyone is working towards a dream. It could be a private dream or something everyone knows about.

It's important to understand that some people's dreams can be riddled with fear. As their friend, colleague and leader you want them to feel good and help them to have less fear in their dreams.

For example, my husband and I started our dental clinic from scratch and it was very difficult to set up our little practice.

We had big dreams and a big vision. But when you have a dream that is so fulfilling and beautiful, it can also come with fear. We experienced fear of not achieving our goals; fear of not knowing what to do in business or how to actually grow a bigger practice and especially fear from wondering what we were going to do if it failed.

We had to harness the **S.T.E.P on Fear** method and follow our own sage advice. That's how I know this works for teams, businesses and organisations. We used it ourselves, every step of the way.

Many people have fears holding them back from their dreams. A writer for example may have a dream to publish their book but the fear of being rejected by publishers and agents stops them from pursuing it. Or an entrepreneur may want to upscale their business but is scared of losing money or not attracting enough clients for the time and effort involved.

Many people forget that even a boss can feel fear. Sometimes the distance between dreams and reality in business is scary. A lot of people are very quick to assume that the boss just makes decisions and doesn't feel real feelings; that it is all about money and not emotional for them. But that isn't true. Bosses also experience fear: fear of not being an effective leader to the fear of their business failing.

Of course no one wants to fail. The worry of failing or not being successful can prevent people from trying. This is how fear can be lurking in your dreams. Yes, your most prized fantasies and visions can also have dark fears prowling in the corners of your mind and soul.

Regardless of their individual job titles, your team will have dreams and fears that are very real to them. Knowing that fear can lurk in other people's dreams too means you can do something about it. It means fear won't take you by surprise.

SETTING OF THE MIND *TEAMS*

In the earlier chapters I introduced **Setting Of The Mind** as the first step to success for yourself. In your role as leader, mentor or friend, now you can help others do the same by applying it to team settings everywhere.

THE ABC'S OF SETTING OF THE MIND *TEAMS*

These stages remain the same as for individuals.

> **A** = Awareness. Acknowledge. Acceptance. Ask.
> **B** = Belonging. Belief. Bonding.
> **C** = Compliment. Confidence. Courage.

A = AWARENESS, ACKNOWLEDGE, ACCEPTANCE AND ASK

All great teams need to begin somewhere. The first step is the foundational step — it sets the firm platform to build from in order to reach great heights. These first four components act as your team's foundation and helps them step higher and higher as they grow.

AWARENESS FOR *TEAMS*

If your team is 'unconscious' and operating on auto-pilot without awareness — then this can lead to disaster. You have to be aware of the whole picture to determine the best course of action. Being mindful and attentive to others is a good trait as a person and especially as a leader, as is being curious and asking questions to improve everyone's awareness.

To **S.T.E.P. on Fear** *Teams*, firstly, you should consider what fears might lurk in the minds of your teams or organisations. From my experience of fears, and my experience of being a leader, team members can have a fear of:
- Talking honestly to their boss or manager
- Confrontation

- Asking for a raise
- Expressing themselves within the group
- Sharing their feelings
- Exposing their weaknesses
- Being seen as incompetent.

Once you are **Aware** of any type of fear within the team, you can then identify it as a problem or challenge that needs to be solved. This can mean talking to your employees or team mates either individually with sensitivity or having an open discussion in a supportive meeting.

Some questions to ask your team could include:
- Do you feel supported by your leaders and colleagues in your role here and as a person?
- How could this be improved on?
- What challenges or problems do you experience here?
- What areas or systems do you think need to change or improve?
- Do you have a dream we could help you achieve?
- What other areas of our organisation require attention?

Answers to these sorts of questions give you a check-in measurement for the health of your team or workplace. Just like the first aid chart that guides you through what to do if you see a person who is unconscious and you follow the ABC's of first aid: check airway, check breathing and check consciousness and circulation of the system.

We can relate that to the life-blood of our team too.

ACKNOWLEDGE FOR *TEAMS*

Closely following **Awareness** is the need to **Acknowledge** the problems or challenges that need to be solved in order to achieve team success and happiness. Ignoring, pretending or putting your head in the sand never works; it just postpones the inevitable fall.

It can be hard for bosses and employees who have been a part of a team for a long time, to **Acknowledge** when things could be done a better way. Remember they might feel fear of the unknown, something we talked about in Part 3.

Discussing and sharing the different perspectives within your team will help everyone to agree and **Acknowledge** when systems need changing and is a very positive signal of development.

Another type of **Acknowledgment** is about owning up to your mistakes, owning up to your role in what happened. Let's look at a simple example. Imagine an employee, 'Karl', who forgot to turn off the air conditioner at the end of the day.

The next morning, another staff member calls out, "Who forgot to turn off the air conditioner yesterday?" Everyone is quiet waiting for the person responsible to answer.

Karl might feel afraid of the consequences of admitting it was his fault and he may choose to lie and say nothing. People then become annoyed and the boss wants to watch the security video to check who was on duty at the time. The negative feelings and consequences will increase if Karl makes the choice to lie.

The alternative is for Karl to actually answer straight away, "I'm sorry. I did it. It was my fault."

This might feel uncomfortable for Karl for a moment but it is so much better than the first scenario where he looked sneaky and guilty and careless. Owning up to his mistake shows his boss he is an honest person.

Karl is a good worker so we can assume this is a rare mistake for Karl to make, and one that he will learn from. His boss may thank him for telling the truth and work out a system so it doesn't happen again by anyone.

If Karl's boss is worried about the extra expense from the air conditioner running all night, then Karl might offer to compensate in some way such as working some extra hours to show he is sorry and wants to add his extra support after the understanding his boss showed him.

Don't be afraid of past failures and don't hang on to them like a bad secret. Burying them deep down can give them more power than they deserve, they were simply an experience to learn from. Be comfortable to talk about your past mistake and what you have learned from it. Don't fall backwards, **Acknowledge** it and move forwards. That shows you are stepping up onto the next level.

Acknowledging the importance of individuals within the team is very important too. **Acknowledge** their hard work, dedication and their contribution. Telling them their help is valued creates a two way street of giving and receiving between the individual and the team. Individuals will want to keep working hard for the group, when their team gives them so much purpose and happiness in return.

ACCEPTING *TEAMS*

Accepting the challenges and accepting your need to resolve them is paramount. Denial of an issue never works, like the toothache I have mentioned before…it only gets worse if you deny it. **Accept** the steps required. Some people think they have accepted something but take no action to move beyond that point. True acceptance means taking the next step in the journey.

The team might decide on a course of action in a meeting and the decision is written down in the meeting records so people know the situation has been accepted and acknowledged. Choose a date to review how the situation is resolving in the near future, and then everyone knows the challenge is being worked on and will be discussed again soon.

ASK FOR HELP *TEAMS*
Once you are **Aware** of the issues that need resolving, have **Acknowledged** what they are and **Accepted** that you must take action, you are ready to **Ask** for help.

Ask your team first for ideas to resolve the challenges from their perspectives. Or **Ask** a business mentor to help you resolve the challenges and grow the business. **Ask** your colleagues for assistance. There is a good chance someone you know has faced similar challenges in their team and has some advice for you to consider if it suits your situation.

Now you are ready for the second stage which emphasises some of the most critical aspects of team success and longevity.

B = BELONGING, BELIEF AND BONDING
Businesses spend large amounts of money trying to create a team that cooperates and shines as one. This starts by caring for the individual and their human needs.

Belonging, Belief and **Bonding** are human needs that must be met so individuals can thrive in any environment or organisation. How well these needs are met can be seen in the culture of the group and creates 'team-think' and team belonging.

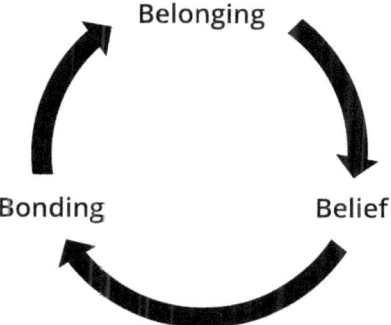

BELONGING *TEAMS*

Developing the 'team-think' of a team and sense of **Belonging** is more than just about team building activities. You need to cultivate a true and deep sense of belonging that makes everyone feel accepted and part of the team. You need to care about each individual within the whole and the whole as one.

Selecting the right team member is giving your team and the new member the best start to their role, a role you hope they are happy in and devoted to for a long time.

However, this can be difficult to achieve. Gallup's 2017 *State of the Global Workplace* report revealed that a whopping 69% of Australian employees are not engaged in their jobs.[1] That is a lot of inefficient time and energy spent by everyone involved.

Everyone does a job to achieve something, even if it's just a job to get money that they immediately spend on clothes or cars, they still have a purpose to showing up to work.

---

[1] Gallup. *State of the Global Workplace* report, (2017) Gallup.com. https://www.gallup.com/workplace/238079/state-global-workplace-2017.aspx

When you hire someone, you need to be selective and figure out their mindset and their reason for wanting the job. Do they actually want to join your team to help build your organisation and share in the dream so it becomes a truly shared vision? Do they want to do well in their role and keep improving their skills, both professional and interpersonal skills?

Select team members in alignment with where you are going so they help steer it in the right direction, with full speed, efficiency and effectiveness. Once you select the right person with the right mindset, put your efforts into sharing your vision, your belief, your goals for the future with them. Give them a copy of your masterplan and include them in the bigger vision.

Another positive thing to try and match up when selecting new team members is to select someone who has similar values to you. For example, when I look for a new employee I need them to operate with three particular values: honesty, trust and transparency.

People feel very comfortable when they are surrounded with honest, transparent people. It allows everyone to operate in a warm environment where they feel safe and treasured. It's important to create an open platform for people to express themselves and share their ideas and give feedback. Creating a positive workplace without gossip or fear helps people feel a sense of belonging and security.

I explain this at the start of the interview process so they have a choice right then, to be honest, to feel comfortable to talk about things, to be transparent, so that we develop trust with each other and within the team. If they are not feeling comfortable with the way our organisation works, that's fine, then there will be another role out there for that person and another person who matches our role.

BELIEF *TEAMS*

The most important aspect of a leader is that they **Believe** in what they are doing. Whether it is a sports team they are coaching, a community group or a workplace, that leader believes their team can achieve their purpose.

This doesn't always mean winning. Think of a sports team who does not win many games because the players bicker and blame one another for things that go wrong.

A caring coach will see the strengths and goodness within each player and will help them become a better teammate. The coach will show them how to support each other and make everyone feel valued. When the players feel good about themselves and their team, often they actually play better because they **Believe** in themselves as a team and enjoy the fun atmosphere and bonds of friendships.

They may not win the grand final but the coach and players can see the extra effort the players have given to the team and they feel the happiness of being part of a close team, it can be a memorable and positive emotional experience playing sport as a team.

Believing is having faith behind your team. You must believe they are the right people for the job, if someone is not the right person you must face up to that fact too, and take action to help them as much as you can. They might have fear of something you didn't understand before.

Your team will feel your **Belief** in them and will be inspired to keep working hard towards your team goal.

BONDING *TEAMS*

It is so important to keep in mind that you are not building your business alone. Remember that your team is building the business and success will be so much sweeter if the team has created lasting memorable **Bonds** with each other along the way.

As a leader, you don't always need to keep your team at a professional distance; the respect and genuine care within work relationships can be very rewarding. In fact, the results of the Harvard Study of Adult Development[2], which began in 1938 and continues to this day, found that happiness was attained through close relationships significantly more than by attaining monetary or social success.

With this in mind and the fact that most people will spend much of their lives at work, doesn't it makes sense to develop our work relationships? To bond with our co-workers that we spend so much time with?

Another report from researchers at BetterUp[3], showed the extra potential from creating a strong sense of belonging within your organisation. It showed that employees who felt this bond:

- Were 50% less likely to quit
- Were more likely to recommend their company
- Took 75% fewer sick days.

It pays to invest in work relationships for your long-term happiness and the success of your business.

You are now ready for the third stage of **Setting of the Mind** *Teams*.

---

2   Original source: George E. Vaillant; Charles C. McArthur; and Arlie Bock, 2010, "Grant Study of Adult Development, 1938-2000", https://doi.org/10.7910/DVN/48WRX9, Harvard Dataverse, V4, UNF:6:FfCNPD1m9jk950Aomsriyg== [fileUNF] Continued study: https://www.adultdevelopmentstudy.org

3   BetterUp Report. 'The value of belonging at work: New frontiers for inclusion.' United States, June 2018. Betterup.com. https://get.betterup.co/rs/600-WTC-654/images/BetterUp_BelongingReport_091019.pdf

C = COMPLIMENT, CONFIDENCE AND COURAGE

These are simple actions and mindsets that play a big part in effective teams. Practise them every day and they will help your team to rise above fear and look down on it.

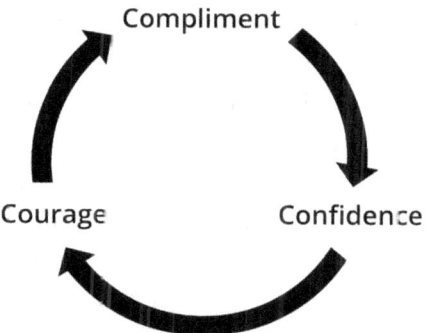

COMPLIMENT *TEAMS*

Praise your team at every opportunity and **Compliment** them on a job well done. The effectiveness of this practice cannot be underestimated when you consider that 79% of employees quit their job due to "lack of appreciation" from their leaders.[4] Take a moment when a hard job is completed, when the budget comes in on track or when a challenge has been overcome, and tell your team in really positive tones what an impressive job they have done and how thankful you are of their efforts.

Well done team
Good job everyone

---

[4] Gallup Business Journal. Robison, Jennifer. "Turning Around Employee Turnover" (Published online, May 8, 2008) Gallup.com. https://news.gallup.com/businessjournal/106912/turning-around-your-turnover-problem.aspx

I'm proud of your efforts
We are kicking goals
Excellent team effort
Keep going

CONFIDENCE *TEAMS*

Compliments for your team help to build a **Confident** team, which becomes a productive team. A **Confident** team mindset is very valuable and gives clients an assurance when they walk through the door that they are in the right place.

Remember to ask team members regularly how they feel and if they have any fears. If you think some people need to build more **Confidence**, offer them extra training to help them feel secure in the application of their knowledge. Often a lack of confidence is not a lack of knowledge, but that the person doesn't feel supported or encouraged to show their full ability and ideas.

COURAGE *TEAMS*

Stemming from this **Confidence**, setting your team's mindset to instil **Courage** is to encourage your team to apply themselves wholeheartedly, to take a leap. Like a curious mind that is scared to travel to all the places they've read about, **Courage** will help them take that first step that will fascinate their senses and empower them to continue.

Team **Courage** can mean many things:
- Encouraging innovation
- Trying new selling methods
- Attempting a new team building activity
- Exploring a new product

Thomas Edison is famous for inventing the light bulb but he admitted he was not successful on his first attempt. In fact it took over 1000 failures before he actually found the right formula and composition for a commercially viable product. If he didn't show **Courage** to keep trying and failing until he succeeded, his name would not be remembered like it is today.

People need to be given space to be **Courageous** and try new opportunities or innovate a new way. I remember reading an interview with Albert Einstein who was asked by a journalist, "What would you be doing if that particular experiment had not succeeded?"

His reply was simply, "You wouldn't be interviewing me now. I would still be doing experiments in the lab until I found the method that worked."

Einstein was committed to his goal and had the **Courage** to simply keep working at it, like a reassurance with determination that it was going to work.

Another form of **Courage** relates to giving and receiving feedback: information given back to the business, team or person. It's a great way to find out what is working and what is not working and make changes accordingly.

Feedback isn't just verbal. Businesses get feedback from a lot of areas: sales, reviews, staff turnover, loss of revenue. To really take in the feedback from staff and customers is an act of **Courage**, because it means you are willing to look at the areas where you can do better and you are open to exploring new territory. A business that takes in constructive feedback with a grateful heart will move forward and accelerate its growth because it evolves to meet with client and staff needs.

To provide the honest feedback to each other in the team is also an act of **Courage** because the leader and the employee can feel vulnerable, they don't know what to expect or what the outcome will be. However as Brené Brown says, "Vulnerability sounds like truth and feels like courage. Truth and courage aren't always comfortable, but they're never weakness." Having the courage to give genuine feedback and feeling safe to have an open conversation in a nurturing workplace is the key to high work performance and business success.

TOOLS *TEAMS*

Tools create the second step, this opens up your team's perspective and potential by utilising three key elements: **Timing, Training** and **Trust**. Just as you can be too scared to step outside your comfort zone and get stuck in the 'compromised zone' as an individual, the same can happen to the team and the business. This zone can really limit your team's perspective and restrain your business growth.

By developing a group culture that is based on the **ABC's of Setting of the Mind** and taking the next higher step so everyone starts to see things from higher ground; they especially begin to notice the new tools, resources and opportunities around them. The right mindset reduces everyone's stressed-out tunnel vision (remember the exercise covering your eyes from Part 3) and opens your vision to what tools and resources are available. Valuable resources come in many forms:

- New software programs
- New pieces of equipment or technology
- Training manuals and company resource material
- Online programs
- Coaching and mentoring
- Your business competitors or sporting and community peers
- Client and customer interaction and feedback
- Research and studies going on in your industry or field

Once you begin to see these tools and resources around you, you become aware of the importance of **Timing** to keep you moving forward towards the team's vision. Each moment is an opportunity to train and improve your team.

You can have the latest equipment and software but if you don't use it at the right time (with the right mindset) it is a waste of time and money.

You need to have clarity and determination, to select the right tool at the right time. This may sound like a spur of the moment decision, but it's not. Once you're operating from a higher perspective, you are constantly looking around for opportunities of growth.

Your team understands this (and is also looking for opportunities) because of this process you've been working through and therefore they understand the reasons for your decision too. Everyone is on the same page and is looking to learn.

Be aware not to get caught up in a moment of enthusiasm and then let it die away. That is like taking one step forward and then two steps back. Carry on with the right **Training** with consistency and persistence and belief — it will transform your team culture, your workplace, your practice, your community!

Training opportunities come in many forms and include hard skill training such as:
- Group training activities
- Workplace inductions and training
- IT and equipment training
- Software systems

And soft skill training in:
- Body language
- Effective communication
- Manner of speech and tone of voice
- Telephone manners
- Sales skills

From the moment you select a team that has similar values to you, when you invest in good **Timing** and **Training**, a beautiful thing is starting to happen as you work together to build one of the most effective elements in a team; **Trust**; or the **Bridge of Trust** as I like to call it. It can't be built without time, training and persistence; it cannot be rushed.

It is amazing to visualise how a bridge is built from connecting two banks together. No matter how far apart the separate banks might be, with effort the connection can happen. In business, there is more than just one **Bridge of Trust**; it is the trust between you and your employees, their trust with each other and importantly the trust between your team and your clients.

Everyone has to work at maintaining their side of the **Bridge of Trust**. The bridge is held in place by the strong faith between you, your team and your clients. Gaining clients'

Trust takes much more than reading facts or testimonials about you, it is more than hearing about your products or services from someone.

Trust is not soundly or solidly built until the customer *experiences* it.

For example, even when they have entered our business and are sitting in the waiting room, our clients are still assessing their choice. They are thinking in their mind, *Did I make the right decision? Are you the person that I should put my trust in? Can I trust you to help me to fix my problem or to handle my concern?*

We must earn and respect their trust the whole way through the process of helping them.

Trust is not to be taken lightly because when **Trust** is broken it is a very deep wound. Even if you try and mend it, there will still be a scar.

> *"It takes 20 years to build a reputation and five minutes to ruin it. If you think about that, you'll do things differently."*
> — Warren Buffet —

Once you destroy **Trust**, you have to work very hard to re-establish it. The scar will remind them of what happened and how they felt. As one of my favourite authors Maya Angelou describes, "People will forget what you say to them and forget what you do, but they will never forget how you made them feel." That is so true in my experience.

Trust in the workplace will pay off abundantly. For example studies have shown the substantial benefits of trust between leaders and their team such as: better performance, greater job satisfaction and lower tendency to want to change jobs.[5] This research also shows that honesty and transparency from leaders, helps employees, "to become more trusting."[6]

Trust is a relationship that must be nurtured just as you nurture a flowerbed, it cannot be ignored and left in the shade without sunlight and water. Only when you actually practise it with all your heart and mind and soul will you see the transformation.

EXAMPLE OF A TOOL USING THE CARE TEMPLATE
TEAMS

Inclusive language in all group situations builds a positive work or team culture. Mindful language also helps your client to experience satisfactory customer service with the 'extra' care. An example of my Care Template below serves as a great tool that helps to resolve conflicts between team members or with customers at work. In fact, you can use the same layout of my Care Template to help resolve any conflicts between people. The best time to resolve a conflict is immediately or as soon as possible. The most effective training method is to follow a tested and proven template. The key to implement this tool successfully is by establishing trust in the relationship.

The flow of my Care Template goes in the following order:
1. Expression of Gratitude followed by a Positive statement

---

5 Black, Hunter. '6 Proven Ways to Create a Culture of Engagement'. Blog post: BetterUp. Retrieved November 2020. Better.com. https://www.betterup.com/en-us/about-us/blog/6-proven-ways-to-create-a-culture-of-engagement

6 Ibid.

2. Inform a situation or concern by starting the sentence with, "Just to let you know…"
3. Suggest a solution and ask for permission to proceed. PAUSE for response.
4. If a response is received with permission, proceed to the next point. If the suggestion is approved, repeat point 2. and 3. with a different approach until an affirmation or permission is obtained to proceed to the next point.
5. Expression of Gratitude for the affirmation/permission/mutual agreement
6. Closing with an appreciation.

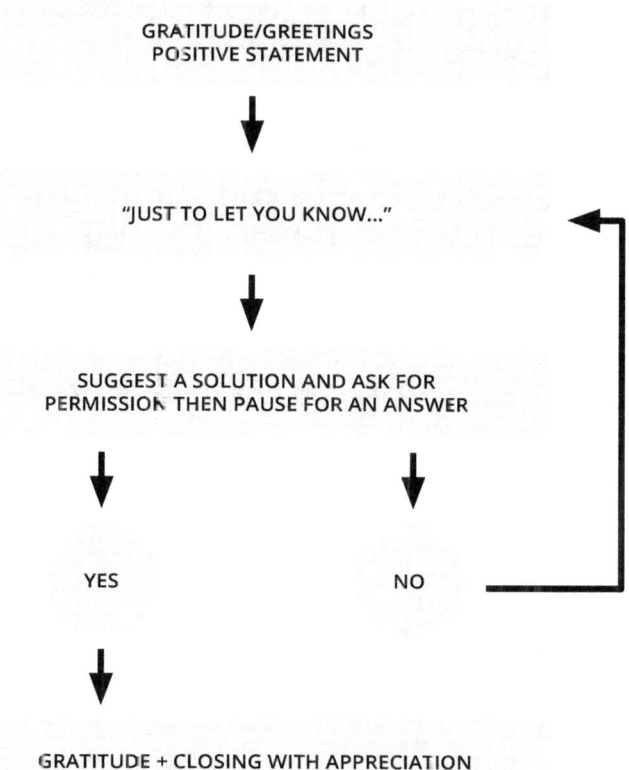

This template is about bringing up a point you want to discuss by firstly engaging the person with a positive statement acknowledging them for listening to you, or asking if it's a good time to talk. Then you say, "Just to let you know…"

You explain the situation and how you think it could be altered or modified and ask them, "What do you think? Is that okay?"

It is very important that you pause and wait for the response and obtain the, "Yes."

If you don't, you need to wait and consider their concerns. Then approach again with a different angle.

Once you reach a mutual agreement, wrap it up positively with gratitude and that you are looking forward to this or that happening.

CASE STUDY 1

A patient calls to request an appointment with Dr A at the clinic where both Dr A and Dr B are equally competent and qualified to help the patient for his treatment needs. Dr A is not available for the next 2 weeks and Dr B is available to see the patient sooner. How would the receptionist answer the patient's call in order to help the patient in a timely manner and fill the appointment book for the business?

> **Patient:** "Hi, I am having a toothache and I want to see Dr A as soon as possible. Is he available tomorrow morning?"
>
> **Receptionist:** "Thank you for calling Chats Dental clinic and certainly I can help you with the booking. Just to let you know that Dr A is not available until 2 weeks, and I

understand you are having a toothache which needs to be looked at as soon as tomorrow morning. May I please book you in with our very experienced Dr B for 10 am tomorrow? Dr B has more than 8 years of experience and you'll be in great hands. May I lock in this very important appointment for you now?"

(PAUSE for patient to respond)

If **Patient** answers, "Sure" then the receptionist can reply as follows.

Receptionist: "Great. I've now secured the appointment for you with Dr B for 10 am tomorrow morning and we are really looking forward to seeing and looking after you."

If **Patient** said, "Who is Dr B? I've never met her. Is she good?"

Receptionist: "Of course. Dr B has been…(give authentic credibility) and is very experienced in (or her expertise is in)…You are in good hands. May I proceed with the booking for you now?"

(PAUSE for patient to respond)

If **Patient** said, "Okay then."

Receptionist: "Great. I've now secured the appointment for you with Dr B for 10 am tomorrow morning and we are really looking forward to seeing and looking after you."

By opening a conversation with gratitude and a positive statement you are welcoming and encouraging the patient to chat with the receptionist about their concern. By letting the patient know of a situation and providing a clear solution followed by a pause to seek the patient's understanding and permission before proceeding, is helping the patient to feel respected and giving them time to recognise your endeavour to help. A closing with gratitude and appreciation is reassuring the patient that they are truly in good care.

On the other hand, if we just tell the patient that we can't book them in because Dr A is not available until two weeks later without giving a good alternative, the patient would not know what to do with their problem, feel lost and deserted and very likely to become more stressed and more anxious. What could be worse is the patient might get too upset to ever return to the clinic. As a result, the business might lose a patient and any further referrals.

This type of issue doesn't just happen in dental clinics, it happens in other businesses too.

CASE STUDY 2

Dental assistant Dora is new to the clinic and when she is stressed, she makes mistakes easily. Dentist Jo speaks fast when she is rushed. When they work together and run over the scheduled time, Jo starts talking too fast for Dora to keep up with her. Mistakes happen as a result and Jo gets angry whilst Dora gets upset. The situation improves when Dora plucks up the courage to use the Care Template for a better understanding of each other.

Dora: Dr Jo, thank you for having me assisting you chairside and I truly enjoy the moments when I can learn great things from you. I just want to let you know that when you speak too fast for me, I can't understand you and I get very nervous and make mistakes. Can you please slow down when you talk to me so that I can do better assisting you to look after the patient?

(PAUSE for Jo's response)

Dr Jo: Oh, I am sorry for stressing you out. That was not my intention. I appreciate having you assist me in taking care of the patients together. I will try to remember to slow down my speech but please do remind me when I speak too fast again. (Smile for recognition).

Dora: Thank you, Dr Jo. I am really looking forward to working alongside you.

Utilising tools with good training in a timely manner is the best way to build trust and establish long-term relationships with the clients and the team.

Whatever system you have in place, make sure you believe in it and that it is well designed to help people. You will find out soon enough if it doesn't work, then you have to acknowledge the system needs to be revised and modified.

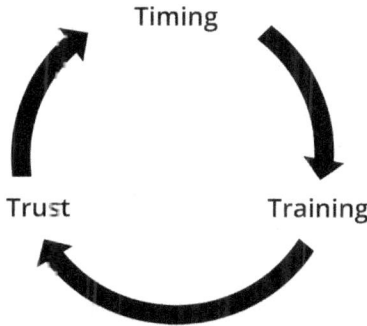

ENJOYMENT *TEAMS*

This part of **S.T.E.P. on Fear** *Teams* is the most exciting:
Emphasis, Experience and **Empowerment** will help you feel the spirit and positive energy surging through your team. This step entwines your own true happiness with how you feel and spend your time at work with other people.

EMPHASIS *TEAMS*

Emphasis is remembering to focus on what truly matters for the team, which is the happiness team members feel from being part of your unique team. The energy and potential of a happy team is magical, people feel supported and strong and a part of something special.

Individuals can become caught up in their own roles and challenges (and successes too) and they can lose contact with the feelings of the rest of the team. Employees start to work independently from one another and they don't look for support or offer support to others.

A star football player is only a star because he's supported by great teammates, both on and off the field. He might be the player who kicked the goal but his teammates created the opportunities for him to shine. His true happiness comes from acknowledging those teammates and **Emphasising** the effort of the whole group.

I witnessed a simple example of individual happiness versus group happiness when my young son, Ethan had his cousins come to our house and they were so excited to play with Ethan's Lego. My son is very proud and protective of his self-designed Lego vehicles and structures. As they played, the younger children would sometimes take a little piece off Ethan's creations, which upset him so much.

Ethan said, "That's mine, you can't take it!"

I explained to Ethan that the fun of playing together is so that everybody can share; sharing is caring. "But it's mine and I want to keep it myself," Ethan replied.

I asked him why he wanted to keep it himself and he said, "Because it makes me happy."

I talked to Ethan about true happiness. That it is not about just being happy by yourself. True happiness is when people around you are happy with you. I helped him to see his cousins were too young to understand the effect of their actions. I suggested that he and I could put the pieces back together after his cousins had gone home, that he and I could repair his Lego together as a fun project. The cousins were happy and Ethan and I were happy as we recreated his wonderful designs later on.

Team happiness at work can also be challenging with many different personalities and work styles. Many of these differences can be reconciled when you start to improve the work culture through the **ABCs of Setting of the Mind**. Things like **Awareness** and **Belonging** and **Compliments** all come together so people start to act and react more positively to each other and feel connected and powerful functioning as a team.

If you know a colleague is working on something difficult and important one day, it could be a report or trying to help a client, it is so nice to remember to ask how they are going the next day and if they would like some help; to remind them they are not in it alone. **Emphasise** the team is behind them.

If there is a negative person in your team, it helps to ask yourself why they might be negative. If you respond to them in a negative way, you have just added to the situation. Could their behaviour be stemming from something they are worried about? Behind the worry, fear could be lurking and if you think they are ready, you could gently help them to unravel and become aware of their fear, using **S.T.E.P. on Fear** *Teams*.

If they are negative all the time perhaps they don't connect with the same values as the team. Don't worry if you have to change staff occasionally, sometimes just being nice and not changing anything is the wrong thing to do.

You can help them understand the team culture you are aiming for, offer them support to stay and work for you and this information will help them decide if your team is the right fit for them. If they leave your team, you have not failed; you are learning and changing for the better every time.

S.T.E.P. on Fear can challenge people's thoughts sometimes, but that is necessary to bring them up to a new level, to change the negative to a positive, it is possible. When we find that team bonding through elevation, the positivity is amplified and even multiplies. It is a ripple effect from your team out into the community; that is how we can make the world a truly better place.

EXPERIENCE *TEAMS*

This involves all the wonderful lessons you learn each day from your interactions with other people. It's a never-ending process but you do become better and better at it as you **Experience** all the different people and situations for your team. Even from moments you did not enjoy at the time, you can be assured you will know better for next time.

I have a personal example to share that was very hard to experience but also one of my greatest lessons that helped me build our wonderful team today.

I once hired a dental assistant when our practice was very small: just me, my husband and this lovely lady who worked very hard for us. Her job was very busy; managing the reception, answering the phone, providing great customer care and she also cleaned our practice until it sparkled.

I was trying to do my best in the technical part, as well as the communication and keeping track of all the follow-ups. It was a tough time for the business because we were so busy but limited in our capacity. We couldn't grow and we couldn't become more viable.

It was difficult to survive balancing all the finances. I was starting to have fear. I was afraid to reach out and ask what we should do differently because of my narrow-mindedness at the time. Along with fear, came frustration, and a lot of other emotions too. Do you know the feeling when any little thing that you see could tick you off? That was me.

The assistant and I still cared for each other and our professions but anger from the fear made me choose some negative words to say. We started to have a lot of arguments and misunderstandings and then the resentment grew. Our words were pushing each other away until one day she resigned. I was only seeing the situation from within my own tunnel vision at the time and when she said she was resigning because her husband was starting a new business interstate, I thought that was the truth.

Only much later, did her husband tell me the truth of it and that she hadn't been able to take the stress anymore but didn't know how to bring it up with me. She didn't want to break my heart, even though I had already broken hers not being an **'Aware'** boss. Even though I loved her, I drove her away, made her so sad and upset. I didn't know how to train my team properly or **Ask** for help for the business.

After she had left I spent so much time trying to find a replacement. So much paperwork and trying to train someone from scratch was so difficult, especially because I wasn't in the right frame of mind. Eventually I decided to employ an experienced lady and pay more. She only stayed for a few months and she left me suddenly without any notice. Her ethics and values had felt very different to mine so we hadn't built that foundation of trust and I hadn't enjoyed working with her as much as my first assistant that I now missed so much.

When she suddenly left (I thought I had no choice and that she should have given me more notice) I felt so devastated from everything I had been through, all the change and uncertainty from the last few months. The next day I decided to lock the clinic so I could go to lunch with some dentist friends, I wanted to vent my anger and frustration out to them.

But while I was at the restaurant something special happened. My old assistant texted me to say she was in Sydney and had come to the clinic to visit me but it was locked. She said she had been wondering how I was going and how all the clients were that we had helped.

She came to the restaurant and when I saw her I couldn't help myself and broke down in tears, so did she. I hugged her and said, "Are you coming back for good? I miss you so much!"

She replied, "Do you need help from me?" She had only been planning on visiting Sydney but after we talked, she was so happy to return.

So I welcomed her back in tears and said, "Thank you so much."

I said our tears were the beginning of joy and we will never shed tears again because of any fear and misunderstanding between us. I was so happy that she cared so much to start work the next day. She believed in me and wanted to give me a second chance.

We had a lot to talk about because I knew I had to hire more staff and she was worried about where she would fit in with this new team and how she would build trust with them, like we had built the trust between us.

She was also worried about hiring a new dentist because she was worried that no one else would care for our clients like we did, but she forgot that we cannot care for everybody in the world. Each client is different and can be cared for in different ways by choosing the right people for the team. We both had to **S.T.E.P. on our Fears**.

The most important thing that we needed to share was our vision, our goal. And that was to help people in need in the way they require. Help people in the way that is the right way, not my way.

This experience helped me open my eyes to the method I had been using in the business. Now I could look at what was happening in the business and what was needed (no fear and better systems) to make people feel confident and happy when they come to work.

I learnt how important it is to look after people, not just sales. How the wrong mindset can have a huge impact on more than just your life, but also on other people's lives. And the right mindset can make positive changes to so many.

Now, I am not scared to go through the hiring process to employ the right person, I'm not scared to let someone go who is not sharing the same dream as me. I used to worry about what people would think. If I did this or that and if I didn't fulfil their needs, if I didn't answer yes to all of their requests so that I was a nice boss.

It is important for you to understand that it's okay to say, "No." And it is even more important for you to know when to say, "Yes!" With courage not fear, when you have learnt what the right thing to do is.

Life is a winding road but you don't have to get hurt at every bump; who says that you cannot dance over the bumps? Who said that you can't create a great song that you can sing along the path of **Experience**?

Be creative, be nurturing, be willing to learn, be motivational, be encouraging, rather than discouraging and be brave to step up to a higher level so that you can see more options open up for you.

EMPOWERMENT *TEAMS*

Empowering your team helps to **Empower** your clients. You can **Empower** everyone to give their best. For our team, we have created a space where clients freely chat about their dental problem and feel assured we can help them. Our solutions not only fix their tooth problem, but also help their life.

They feel transformed, they feel encouraged, they feel energised, they feel recharged, they feel fulfilled, they feel so happy that they are part of our team, yes; even our clients are part of our team. So for me, I am proud that we provide an A plus service so they can chat freely about their problem or problems.

When our clients first come to us, we put forth our best efforts to earn their confidence and trust so they know their problem is going to be identified and addressed. The added value is that they are surprised when they learn more about how to enrich their life and even address their life problems in the dental clinic. Just like serving Mr Phillips his cup of ginger tea that day; it slowed him down from the stressed pace of his life and he was surprised how much he was looking forward to coming to see his dentist.

Always be present with the **ABCs of Setting the Mind**, followed by the implementation of the three Ts of **Tools**: the **S.T.E.P. on Fear** model helps you choose specific words and use strategic phrases at the right time. The result can be so powerful and for us, it gives our clients a sense of ease and relief when they choose to come into our care. This is one thing that is very special about us. You can do the same.

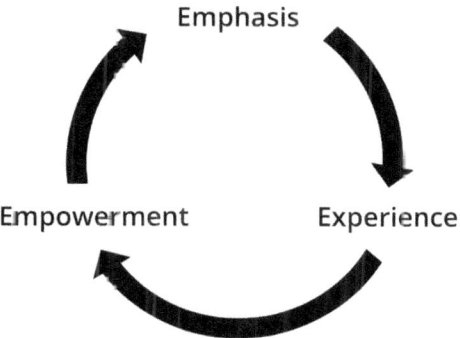

Dealing effectively with conflict, doubt and different types of feedback builds **Empowerment**, this leads to improved relationships with friends and family, colleagues and clients, regardless of age, gender, cultural and generational differences.

When systems are in place, life becomes better in so many situations. Systems help to avoid people taking the easy way; in my experience 'easy' can make people lazy. Don't complicate problems further; you can become overwhelmed and exhausted. Your judgement becomes clouded; your fear can make you feel like you're suffocating.

So instead of actually complicating it, delaying it, ignoring it or trying to fight all alone by yourself – you should identify the real problem, recognise it and find help and use the right tools. Use a simple formula so you can feel empowered and enjoy the process of solving it.

It can be hard to acknowledge but if you don't simplify it, you might be the one who is actually adding to the issue that has such a big impact on everyone.

PURPOSE *TEAMS*

It is vitally important to know why you're in business. To ask what is your deeper **Purpose**?

Simon Sinek put it so well in his 2009 TED Talk, "People don't buy what you do, they buy *why* you do it." More than ever before, people want to engage with a business that cares. A business that is more than just profiting.

In 2019 Microsoft launched a project called, *The Art of Teamwork* whose research showed the number one requirement for successful teams is to have a clear team **Purpose**. It said **Purpose** creates, "shared meaning, which keeps teams focused, aligned and performing at a peak level."[7]

With so much easily accessible information available on the internet, people seek more than just product details, services provided, or price comparisons when making a decision on what to purchase. They want to know the values and mission and vision of a company. They want to know if it's environmentally friendly, if the products they use are

---

[7] Microsoft 2019. 'The Art of Teamwork: fostering healthy team dynamics to drive innovation and business success.' https://www.microsoft.com/en-au/microsoft-365/microsoft-teams/teamwork-in-the-workplace?ocid=AID2484862_QSG_373700&rtc=1

ethical. They want to know why you're in business.

The public demands more honourable and responsible businesses now and so they should. A leader should believe in their business and their employees should see their passion shine through each day.

Your team must know your 'business mission' that summarises its **Purpose** and goals and how it will achieve them.

Your team should also know your 'business vision', which summarises the company's hopes for the long-term future once it fulfils its mission.

Together, your business mission and vision help you to create your Business Purpose Statement. Similar to a Purpose Statement for an individual, a Business Purpose Statement can serve for a shorter period of time to help focus team efforts towards the closest goal you are all aiming towards.

For example, a short-term statement could concentrate on growth such as, 'Thirty new clients in 30 days' or you might be focusing on strengthening your connection with clients, 'Phone clients that you haven't heard from in 12 months'. A sports team might write in their newsletter, 'Encourage each other to have another go'.

These statements help the team to stay focused on their goal as they work through their daily tasks.

Create a new Business Purpose Statement once that goal is reached, or even if that goal needs to be re-evaluated if unforeseen obstacles occurred. These obstacles may have created some frustrations or fears within the team and this shows why the **S.T.E.P. on Fear *Teams*** process is always relevant as a check-in method on the team's health and happiness.

Fears can arise in individuals and employees from so many different directions, interactions with people and from experiences in their past.

Checking in regularly with your team using the **S.T.E.P. on Fear model for *Teams*** will help to create the wonderful feeling of engagement the employee or individual is looking for to achieve fulfilment in their life.

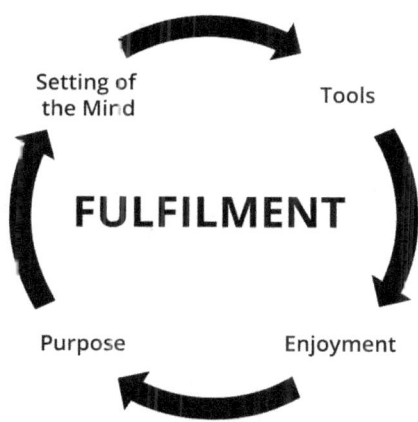

EMBED A GIVING MODEL INTO YOUR BUSINESS

Our business purpose is an extension of our purpose in life: to help other people from a place of love. We were excited for our business, Chats Dental to become a 'better business' through the B1G1 program that I introduced in Part 3.

This program helps businesses to create meaningful impacts around the world. Our team and our customers can feel the joy of giving back to the world just because of the relationship we have in business together; it's all connected!

Our giving model is simple and exemplifies how any business can integrate actions that make a difference into their corporate ethos. Their passion and love can flow on to others less fortunate in tangible ways.

We have been able to contribute to many of the United Nations' Sustainable Development Goals (SDGs), however SDG 10, *Reducing Inequality* is the goal our business supports the most. As mentioned earlier in Part 2, we feel privileged to be able to offer the following as part of our contribution to the United Nations SDGs:

- When a new patient appointment is made, we provide one daily dose of vitamin A supplements to a child in Turkana, Kenya.
- When a client accepts a cup of tea or coffee at reception, we provide one day's worth of grain to nourish a child in Malawi.
- When we see a client for emergency care, we plant a tree to support reforestation in Borneo.
- When we provide painless dentistry using IV sedation, we give a meal to a rescued animal through Edgar's Mission in Victoria, Australia.
- When a new child sits in the dental chair, happily counting teeth with us, we provide one day of education support to a disadvantaged child in New Zealand.
- When a client laughs in the dental chair and thanks us for an enjoyable dental experience, we provide one day of access to personal hygiene to a girl in Kenya or Nepal.
- When a client returns for their six-month dental check-up, we provide one day of access to dental hygiene to a child in El Jebha, Morocco.
- When a client's smile is transformed by functional aesthetics, four rainforest trees are planted and protected

to help the survival of the southern cassowary at Mission Beach in Queensland, Australia.
- When we perform the Chats Dental Puppet Show to educate pre-schoolers and school children, we give one special learning tool to a child in Buffalo City, South Africa.
- When we give out a *Certificate of Gratitude* to a valued client, we give one day of access to reading materials to a girl in Cambodia.

We believe that giving is not just about what it does for others, it is also about what it does for us, making our business both meaningful and purposeful. These small actions make a difference to disadvantaged people in many countries by improving access to healthcare and education, providing better opportunities and employment, and reminding us that we are all connected, valued and loved.

LEAVING A LEGACY

The core of this book is love; in love there is no fear. Love is something that you can magnify and amplify and pass on. It is up to each person to pass on the wisdom they have learned to the next generation. I see this as my duty and blessing to be able to share what I have learned.

My father wanted to lift his family out of the hardships of poverty and misery that he and his relatives had known for so many decades since the war. He saw education as the key to changing his family's future. He was very fortunate that he had some really wonderful teachers and mentors that wanted to see his eyes light up with joy when he was given the opportunity to learn and to be educated.

We did not become a wealthy family by western standards. But we always felt fortunate. I could see the beauty in the hard work of my parents to provide shelter, health, safety and education. They wanted to see me receive this happiness. They were happy *for* us but I don't think they knew they could also have happiness for themselves.

Now I'm a parent and I have learnt so much from my parents and my own experiences. For a time I also thought I would be happy if my kids can have this or that. I thought *I am working hard for their happiness just like my parents worked for mine.*

If I felt that moment of sadness, or disagreement or disapproval, I would shut myself off into my little dark corner and think that there's nothing I could do about it. I told myself, *I am sacrificing happiness because this is for my children.*

One day a voice said, *What about me? What about my relationship with my husband? What about my relationship with my parents, with my in-laws, with my colleagues, with my business, with society, with the community, and even with the world?* I felt we were all connected and I wanted to help everyone, including myself.

What eyes cannot see, the mind cannot recognise. I had a limiting belief that created tunnel vision and a narrow mindset with the fear of failing to provide happiness for my kids. Changing my mindset from scarcity to abundance and using fear as my foundation to step higher, gave me a new perspective — to visualise my life with meaning and to create the legacy I want to leave. Once you grow in that mindset of abundance, you will be driven to propagate those teachings to other people because of the joy you experience as you unfold your true self with unlimited possibility.

It is like the incredible migration of the monarch butterflies that take many generations to complete their return journey.

They hold on to a deep, instinctive knowledge of their path, their connection and their purpose.

In today's time, with fear all around us, many people feel they can just blow away in the wind. But like the monarch butterflies' inner strength, I want to show people they can have deep meaning to their life and be unshakeable, even in the face of fear.

My S.T.E.P. formula can help you to realise, *Hey, I don't have to run away from fear. I don't have to hide; I can face it step by step.*

I want to provide this wisdom, not as a leader to follow but as someone who is still in the process with you. If you are suffering in a dark hole, then I want to show you the way up into the light. In fact we can do it together, it is not a single narrow staircase.

Once you see the opportunities, the resources and tools around you, you can live larger than your current life. This is not greedy or selfish, it is your own beautiful growth and something to share and teach to others.

In our practice, we aim to nurture and help everybody. We hope every day our team looks forward to coming to work. We want to give each person something that adds value to their life. We overflow with abundance to share with our team and our clients.

For example, we once recruited a new receptionist to join our team, knowing that she was looking for a short term career opportunity before pursuing her dream of becoming a lawyer. Whilst appreciating her honesty and acknowledging her keenness to learn about helping people during the interview, we took her in and provided her with the training in personal and professional development skills. When she was offered an opportunity to work in a big law firm, we gave her a wholehearted farewell marked by mixed feelings of sadness for her leaving and happiness for her entering a new phase. What happened in her beautiful story was that she returned to us.

> Here is an excerpt from her heartfelt email to us:
> *I had a blast working with you guys and I love everything that you stand for. Working for a small business is so different to working for a big law firm where there are over 600 employees. I want to see Chats Dental grow and I want to be able to be a part of that. I want to remain committed to you guys, through thick and thin because you are like a family to me and we support each other.*
> ...
> *Who knows what the future holds, but for now, I know where I belong is with you.*
> ...
> *I want you to know that from the deepest part of my heart, I want to be a part of the team again.*

You can step up to be who you want to be and do what you want to do, without fear. Take action; and turn dreams into reality, you won't look back and your joy will overflow into a beautiful legacy for so many others, who will in turn help even more people find strength in joy and love to overcome fear; it's a wonderful never-ending process.

Now it is time to change your life and **S.T.E.P. on Fear**!

> Everything you want is on the other side of fear.
>
> **JACK CANFIELD**

ACKNOWLEDGEMENTS

I am wholeheartedly thankful to my dear parents, Victor and Amy, who raised me with their unconditional love and brought my brother, Eric and I the greatest gift in life of knowing God. Because of His faithfulness and amazing grace, I am who I am today.

To my loving husband, Robert, I am so grateful to your never-ending support. I feel so blessed to have your shoulder to lean on, your heart to comfort and your wisdom to share. To our beautiful children, Sarah and Ethan, thank you for loving me just the way I am and always helping me to stay positive.

To my mentors:

Paul Dunn and Masami Sato (b1g1.com) — Thank you for showing me that meaningful impacts are created by the collective power of small!

Sam and Kate Cawthorn (speakersinstitute.com) — Thank you for guiding me on the path to follow my passion and to find my voice.

Tracey Williams, Tanya Hill, Carl Porter and the team of Align Technology — Thank you for taking me with you on a journey to create millions of smiles around the world!

All my school teachers, classmates, fellow alumni in Taiwan and in Australia — Thank you for shaping me into a person with resilience, strength and compassion.

To my colleagues in the dental industry and my valued clients — Thank you for teaching me the importance of staying connected in both good and tough times.

To Ting, Kayla, Justine, Annabel, and my awesome team at Chats Dental — Thank you for believing in me and sharing our vision together to make a difference in people's lives.

To Susan Dean, Natalie Deane and the Dean Publishing team — Thank you for your enormous efforts and unlimited support. Without you, my book ideas would still be floating in the air. Because of you, this book can be held in the hands and close to the hearts of those near and far. Thank you for helping me to amplify the joy of reading and to magnify the purpose in life whilst knowing how to **S.T.E.P. on Fear**!

ABOUT THE AUTHOR

Dr Catherine Yang is an author, speaker, dentist, and business owner.

Serving as a dentist since the age of 24, Dr Catherine Yang is dedicated to helping people manage fear effectively. Coupled with powerful case studies and tangible takeaways, Catherine's book and presentations will empower you to unlock what is needed to **S.T.E.P. on Fear** and steer your life to success and joy.

Catherine is a member of the Australian Dental Association, a fellow of the International College of Continuing Dental Education, a past secretary of Northern Suburbs Dental Study Group, a facilitator of the International College of Dental Practitioners, a keynote speaker, and published a clinical white paper for Invisalign Australia.

Catherine is also a member of B1G1 and provided a story for the publication of *LEGACY: The Sustainable Development Goals in Action*. Her latest book *S.T.E.P on Fear* has been described as "the perfect blend of action and awareness in our fear-driven world."

To find out more about Catherine or book her as a speaker for your event or team workshop, go to:

steponfear.com
drcatherineyang.com
chatsdental.com.au

TESTIMONIALS

"I heard Catherine speak about stepping on fear — S.T.E.P — Step On Fear. That resonated with me. Fear was my mountain, but I saw that mountain and I took it on! Because that's all fear is! If you can step over it, step by step, layer upon layer, you're going to rise above it and then fear will become very miniscule from that higher perspective. You have to break that mind barrier to overcome it. Catherine teaches that."

Khoa Nam Tran
Speaker and author of *Legless to Legless*

"I'm Brad Twynham, a performance coach to executives and elite entrepreneurs. I just saw Dr. Catherine Yang speak and I've got to tell you she is one of the most engaging and informative speakers I've seen in a long time. I learned so much from her talk. It was just unbelievable. If you get a chance to see her — come along, Catherine is absolutely amazing!"

Bradley Twynham
Performance coach and Investment Committee Chair at Scale Australia Investing

"I've just heard Catherine Yang speaking today at the Speakers Institute. Absolutely amazing! If you ever get the opportunity to hear her speak, she'll leave you speechless. She has an amazing smile and she's so inspirational and motivational. Dr. Catherine Yang — I wish you all the best and I really look forward to seeing you on the world stage again. God bless you. Thank you."

Rita Barbagallo
Author of *Magic and Miracles*, Director of The Red Peacock, Founder of Barbee Barb Children's Entertainment & Magic School, Chair of HerStory Women's Global Empowerment Conference in Sydney 2019

"I have just had the absolute pleasure to see Dr. Catherine Yang on stage delivering an amazing presentation about stepping on fear. As a dentist, she has experienced many people having fear of visiting the dentist. And she has transformed that message to be a life lesson for people. She has a formula to be able to help you step on your fears. Catherine would be an absolutely fantastic speaker at your next event."

Dianne McCabe
Director and Change Coach of "The Happy Path"

"I've just seen Catherine Yang onstage presenting how to change your life and the steps involved to make a real difference. I was blown away by her genuine authenticity. Her message is amazing. I even took notes and I'm going to implement the changes she talks about within 24 hours (she knows you must implement within 24 hours). So if you want to change anything within your life, you need to follow the steps that Catherine puts in place for you. So if you get the opportunity to have Catherine in your proximity, whether that be in a professional environment, or social environment, make sure you catch up with her and get her to help you to make change in your life."

Warren Tate
MC and Presentation Coach

"Hi, my name is Ruth. I'm a Gallup certified coach and own a consulting procurement agency. I had the pleasure of listening to Cath talk in an interview with Sam Cawthorn and she talked about stepping on fear. She talked about breaking down fear into very simple easy-to-understand S.T.E.P — Step on Fear! It's so easy to understand. It's so easy to apply. So thank you Cath. I recommend all to listen to Cath speak. Thank you."

Ruth Saw
Procurement Specialist at Blu Dot Consultancy, Author of *Clarity Is Power*, Gallup Certified Strengths Coach

"Hi, my name is YP Lai. I'm the owner and founder of 7 Secrets Life Balance System. And I was working with Catherine at the protege program and you know what? I'm really, really so impressed with her. Why? Because she shows her hard work, her commitment or wanting to deliver a message.

No, she's not just a dentist, she is somebody with a passion that wants to help people to overcome fear. Her message was so simple, so clear, because she has put in the effort to make it easy, simple for people to understand and able to execute it. So ladies and gentlemen, I recommend you go and talk to Catherine and find out about her S.T.E.P system — Step on Fear. She's the best. Thank you."

YP Lai
Founder of 7 Secrets Life Balance System,
National Director at BNI Thailand, BNI Vietnam, BNI Korea and BNI Philippines, Senator of Junior Chamber International

NOTES

STEP ON FEAR

ENDNOTES

PART 1
1. Russell, Bertrand. *Unpopular Essays*. (1950), George Allen & Unwin, London.
2. Dr Dorothy Brougham http://www.ortv.com/en/dr-doris-brougham
3. Studio Classroom http://www.studioclassroom.com/h_doris.php

PART 2
1. Russell, Bertrand. *Unpopular Essays*. (1950), George Allen & Unwin, London.
2. Fossion P Rejas MC, Servais L, Pelc I, Hirsch S (2003). "Family approach with grandchildren of Holocaust survivors". *American Journal of Psychotherapy*. 57 (4): 51927. doi:10.1176/appi.psychotherapy.2003.57.4.519. PMID 14735877.
3. Pew Research Center. "Greatest Dangers in the World". Washington, D.C. (October 16, 2014). https://www.pewresearch.org/global/2014/10/16/greatest-dangers-in-the-world.

4. Boston Children's Hospital. "Phobias, Symptoms and Causes". Retrieved online 2nd Sept 2020. http://www.childrenshospital.org/conditions-and-treatments/conditions/p/phobias/symptoms-and-causes

5. Australian Institute of Health and Welfare 2018. Australia's health 2018. Australia's health series no. 16. AUS 221. Canberra: AIHW. https://www.aihw.gov.au/getmedia/7c42913d-295f-4bc9-9c24-4e44eff4a04a/aihw-aus-221.pdf)

6. LaMontagne AD, Sanderson K, & Cocker F (2010): Estimating the economic benefits of eliminating job strain as a risk factor for depression: summary report. Victorian Heath Promotion Foundation (VicHealth), Melbourne, Australia. https://www.vichealth.vic.gov.au/~/media/ResourceCentre/PublicationsandResources/Economic%20participation/Job%20strain/P-022-SC_Job_Strain_SUMMARY_October2010_V12.ashx)

7. Angelou, M., 2016. *Caged Bird Legacy | The Legacy Of Dr. Maya Angelou.* [online] Retrieved 14 March 2016. http://www.mayaangelou.com

8. https://www.tinyhabits.com/about

PART 3

1. Martin, Patrick. "The epidemiology of anxiety disorders: a review." *Dialogues in clinical neuroscience* vol. 5,3 (2003): 281-98. https://www.ncbi.nlm.nih.gov/pmc/articles/PMC3181629/?xid=PS_smithsonian

2. Harvard Medical School, 2007. National Comorbidity Survey (NCS). (2017, August 21). Retrieved from https://www.hcp.med.harvard.edu/ncs/index.php. Data Table 1: Lifetime prevalence DSM-IV/WMH-CIDI disorders by sex and cohort

3. ABC News. Lloyd, Shelley. "Phobias of fish, spiders among 'irrational' fears for up to 15pc of population". Published online Tuesday 3 December 2019. https://www.abc.net.au/news/2019-12-03/phobias-a-risk-for-15-per-cent-of-

population/11734718

4. Carleton, R. Nicholas. (2016). Fear of the Unknown: One Fear to Rule them All?. *Journal of Anxiety Disorders*. Page 39-41. https://doi.org/10.1016/j.janxdis.2016.03.011

5. Rein G, Atkinson, M, McCraty R. "The Physiological and Psychological Effects of Compassion and Anger", *Journal of Advancement in Medicine*. 1995; 8(2): 87-105.. https://www.heartmath.org/research/research-library/basic/physiological-and-psychological-effects-of-compassion-and-anger/

6. Verduyn, P., Lavrijsen, S. "Which emotions last longest and why: The role of event importance and rumination". *Motiv Emot* 39, 119–127 (2015). https://doi.org/10.1007/s11031-014-9445-y. https://link.springer.com/article/10.1007%2Fs11031-014-9445-y#citeas

7. Steve Furtick, Facebook, 27th October, 2015.

8. Housman, Michael, and Dylan Minor. "Toxic Workers." Harvard Business School Working Paper, No. 16-057, October 2015. http://nrs.harvard.edu/urn-3:HUL.InstRepos:23481825

9. Cameron, K., Mora, C., Leutscher, T., & Calarco, M. (2011). Effects of Positive Practices on Organizational Effectiveness. *The Journal of Applied Behavioral Science*, 47(3), 266–308. https://doi.org/10.1177/0021886310395514

10. Seligman, M. E. F., Steen, T. A., Park, N., & Peterson, C. (2005). Positive Psychology Progress: Empirical Validation of Interventions. *American Psychologist*, 60(5), 410–421. https://doi.org/10.1037/0003-066X.60.5.410

11. Sugawara SK, Tanaka S, Okazaki S, Watanabe K, Sadato N (2012) Social Rewards Enhance Offline Improvements in Motor Skill. *PLoS ONE* 7(11): e48174. https://doi.org/10.1371/journal.pone.0048174

12. Theodore Roosevelt 'Citizenship in a Republic' (Speech at the Sorbonne, Paris, April 23, 1910)

13. Cambridge dictionary online. 2020. Available at <https://dictionary.cambridge.org/dictionary/english/empowerment> (Accessed 17 September 2020).
14. Hur M.H. (2013) Empowerment. In: Gellman M.D., Turner J.R. (eds) *Encyclopedia of Behavioral Medicine*. Springer, New York, NY
15. Page, N., & Czuba, C. E. (1999). Empowerment: What is it? *Journal of Extension*, 37(5), 24–32.

PART 4

1. Gallup. *State of the Global Workplace* report, (2017) Gallup.com. https://www.gallup.com/workplace/238079/state-global-workplace-2017.aspx
2. Original source: George E. Vaillant; Charles C. McArthur; and Arlie Bock, 2010, "Grant Study of Adult Development, 1938-2000", https://doi.org/10.7910/DVN/48WRX9, Harvard Dataverse, V4, UNF:6:FfCNPD1m9jk950Aomsriyg== [fileUNF] Continued study: https://www.adultdevelopmentstudy.org
3. BetterUp Report. 'The value of belonging at work: New frontiers for inclusion.' United States, June 2018. Betterup.com. https://get.betterup.co/rs/600-WTC-654/images/BetterUp_BelongingReport_091019.pdf
4. Gallup Business Journal. Robison, Jennifer. "Turning Around Employee Turnover" (Published online, May 8, 2008) Gallup.com. https://news.gallup.com/businessjournal/106912/turning-around-your-turnover-problem.aspx
5. Black, Hunter. '6 Proven Ways to Create a Culture of Engagement'. Blog post: BetterUp. Retrieved November 2020. Better.com. https://www.betterup.com/en-us/about-us/blog/6-proven-ways-to-create-a-culture-of-engagement
6. Ibid.
7. Microsoft 2019. 'The Art of Teamwork: fostering healthy team dynamics to drive innovation and business success.'

https://www.microsoft.com/en-au/microsoft-365/microsoft-teams/teamwork-in-the-workplace?ocid=AID2484862_QSG_373700&rtc=1

www.ingramcontent.com/pod-product-compliance
Lightning Source LLC
Chambersburg PA
CBHW071616080526
44588CB00010B/1155